S0-BDP-312

RIGHTS

RIGHTS
BUYING. PROTECTING. SELLING

Petra Christine Hardt

Written in collaboration with
Nora Mercurio, Christoph Hassenzahl,
Manuel Quirin and Janika Rüter

TRANSLATED BY
JEREMY GAINES, LUCY RENNER JONES
AND RICHARD STOIBER

LONDON NEW YORK CALCUTTA

Seagull Books 2011

Buying, Protecting and Selling Rights: Wie urheberrechtlich geschützte Werke erworben, gesichert und verbreitet werden

© Bramann Verlag, Frankfurt am Main 2008

First published in English by Seagull Books, 2011

English translation © Jeremy Gaines, Lucy Renner Jones and Richard Stoiber, 2011

ISBN-13   978 0 8574 2 003 9

British Library Cataloguing-in-Publication Data
A catalogue record for this book is available
from the British Library

Typeset by Seagull Books, Calcutta, India

Printed and bound by Hyam Enterprises, Calcutta, India

CONTENTS

	Foreword	*vii*
1	BUYING RIGHTS	1
1.1	Direct domestic authors' contract	3
1.1.1	Contract subject matter and contract partners	8
1.1.2	Print run, retail price, availability and the possibility of an author withdrawing	12
1.1.3	Royalties and advance payments	15
1.1.4	Subsidiary rights	18
1.1.5	Electronic rights	22
1.1.6	The option clause	24
1.1.7	Termination of the author's contract	25
1.2	Contracts with foreign authors via an agent or a foreign publishing house	25
2	PROTECTING RIGHTS	33
2.1	The dialogue with the author	34
2.2	Maintenance of the work following the author's death	43
3	SELLING RIGHTS	49
3.1	Selling translation rights	49
3.1.1	Market and sector knowledge	54
3.1.2	Intermediaries	57
3.1.3	Strategies	63
3.2	Use of print subsidiary rights in the domestic market	69

3.2.1	Paperback editions	70
3.2.2	Book club editions	73
3.2.3	Special editions	74
3.2.4	Own print versus licensed edition	76
3.3	Administration	78
4	**BOOK PUBLISHING IN THE DIGITAL AGE**	81
4.1	E-books	81
4.2	Open access	85
4.3	New and established duties	86
5	**APPENDICES**	
	Appendix A A Sample Royalty Scale	88
	Appendix B A Few Sample Contracts	90
	1. Author Contract	90
	1A. Author Contract Addendum For E-Rights	107
	2. Suhrkamp Licence Agreement	111
	Appendix C Some Useful Websites	126
	Appendix D Suggested Reading	128

The starting point for the following four essays was a series of lectures, and the questions that arose from the audience confirmed with certainty that the acquisition and protection of rights, as carried out by small, medium-sized and independent European publishing houses, are topics of interest in other markets too. These essays are generally intended for those who are entrusted with establishing rights and royalty departments in Asia, Arab countries and Africa.

A further aspect also came to light during the lectures: that the changes to which rights trading has been subject over the last 20 years and the perspectives resulting from these make this a favourable time to take stock of the situation.

PROTECTING INTELLECTUAL PROPERTY
IN THE DIGITAL AGE

The discussion between authors and publishers on
contract periods and appropriate remuneration,
disputes between publishing houses and Internet
providers regarding the use of digitized texts and
the simultaneity of print and e-books should be
based on an acknowledgement of the fact that the
acceleration mechanisms of international markets
have wrought enormous changes in the publishing
industry.

In this context I would like to highlight the
responsibility of 'publishing houses as navigators in
the cultural industry', a phrase that Gottfried
Honnefelder, the head of the German Publisher's
Association, used at a speech, thereby placing the
bilateral relationship between copyright owner and
publisher in a larger social context.

This topic has become an explosive issue
because governments and renowned institutions
have recently spoken out in favour of the free use of
copyright-protected works in public institutions,
libraries and museums. Such use affects the legal
systems in which the right of ownership gives
equal value to intellectual and physical property. In
its exemplary function, this equal rank is imperative for global rights trading. The response to an

easing of the protection afforded to rights can only be to make the bond even closer between the author and publisher, the copyright holder and user. Despite the enthusiasm for open access, I believe we should not forget that it has been standard practice for centuries to pay the author for his printed work. It is a matter for debate whether this also calls for the obligation to compensate him to the same extent for use of his works in digital form.

Robert Darnton, Director, Harvard Library and renowned book historian, describes the advantages of unlimited free access to the results of Harvard research in an interview with German journalist Jordan Mejias, thereby making a comparison between the upheaval in the history of communication methods and Gutenberg's invention. Three factors for this upheaval are discussed below.

TECHNOLOGICAL PROGRESS

The first factor relates to technological progress: the resulting changes in the requirements of media use and knowledge transfer as well as an increased frequency of demand caused by globally operating equipment manufacturers present a new challenge for publishing houses.

E-books have rapidly become a fixed market segment and turnover factor beside printed books since 2009 after initial investments by publishing houses in the digitization of organic book stock. With increasing experience from publishers and aggregators, efficient equipment in terms of both design and technology has existed since the beginning of 2010. The limits of conventional reading are being expanded and, in some cases, revolutionized. Changes have affected two inseparable aspects: technical features, in particular the creation of new, interrelated user possibilities of media content; and the resulting definition of 'conditions of use' together with their legal, administrative and financial aspects.

Nevertheless, it is imperative to increase awareness among booksellers, manufacturers and readers too, that the intellectual output and economic efforts invested by publishers in such products is the same as for printed books.

ACCELERATION IN GLOBAL RIGHTS TRADING

Prior to 1989, rights trading occurred only between Western Europe, the US, South America, Israel and Japan. Following the political opening of the private sector in Eastern Europe, publishing houses emerged in 18 Central and Eastern European countries, replacing state publishing houses which, until 1989, held exclusive rights to publish foreign literature and academic works. On 15 October 1992, the People's Republic of China acceded to the Berne Convention. And two weeks later, on 30 October 1992, to the Universal Copyright Convention. Between 1992 and 1995, other Asian, Arab and African states followed suit, and it is only from this point that we can talk about global rights trading. The period of time from which rights of use were transferred from copyright owner to publisher, and were protected worldwide by contract, has therefore been relatively short and represents a unique historic caesura for the entire book industry. The absence for decades of legal trade relations in many markets and the subsequent neglect of copyright protection has been swiftly replaced by an acceleration in rights trading which cannot always do justice to the value of literature and academic works.

INCREASED INFLUENCE OF LITERARY AGENCIES

The third factor in the transformation of the manufacturing book trade is the growth in influence of literary agencies. In some cases, these agencies are not sufficiently informed about the production process and the immense costs that a publishing house has to manage on a daily basis. Encouraged by the ever-faster operating book market, some agencies make irresponsible demands for advances which are never recuperated through book sales and subsidiary rights, thus endangering the independence of smaller publishing houses. By negotiating a contract with a publishing house, the agent assumes a function otherwise performed by the publishing house without bearing the latter's publishing risk. This is only advisable and justified if the agent considers itself a partner of both the author and the publishing house.

CHALLENGES FOR THE BOOK MARKET

All three factors taken together—changes due to the digital use of copyright-protected works; the internationalization of the book market; and the increased influence of agencies in the author–publisher relationship—have increased the challenges for publishers in the international book market.

In many publishing houses, the acquisition of rights, the issue of authors' contracts, control over royalties and the sale of foreign rights or the execution of subsidiary rights in the domestic market are functionally separate. By way of contrast, my explanations assume that the administrative responsibility for the three main functions in the field of rights, namely buying, protecting and selling, is a single entity. In order to avoid misunderstandings, I would like to emphasize quite clearly that with the term 'buying rights' I am not referring to decisions with regard to the publishing programme. This must be reserved for the publisher. Colleagues in rights departments can, however, contribute to this decision with their knowledge of appropriate advances, royalty scales, contract periods, catalogues of subsidiary rights and publication deadlines. The closer the union between programme management and rights departments, the more beneficial it is in terms of the company's earnings and its use in long-term publishing plans.

Precision, contractual knowledge, market knowledge, strategic thinking in rights departments and joint future planning by the publisher, editorial team and rights manager are prerequisites for the submission of appropriate contract proposals to the author and the guarantee of realizing contractual content that meets the author's expectations. In international licensing deals, joint responsibility for the structure of the contract when buying rights and the exploitation of such rights lead to important transparency in the respective market.

HOW TO USE THIS BOOK

The first chapter is devoted to an interpretation of the author's contract with regard to those points relevant to the long-term safeguarding of rights and as such lead to Chapters Two and Three, which are intended to provide guidance on the practice of maintaining a backlist and disseminating print rights at home and abroad.

My explanations are intended to serve as a basis for discussion and a recollection of contractual values, which, in the experience of several independent publishing houses, form the basis of the unique relationship between author and publishing house and guarantee the economic success of both. The duties of the publishing house, namely to help authors attain economic independence, establish an international readership and keep the work available even after their death, are the direct result of the author's contract. They ensure the economic independence of the copyright owner and user.

The following explanations are related to practice and are based on my professional duties at Suhrkamp. For 50 years, Siegfried Unseld, publisher (1959–2002), and Helene Ritzerfeld, Rights Director (1950–2000), successfully negotiated authors' contracts for Suhrkamp Verlag, Insel, Jüdischer Verlag and Deutscher Klassiker Verlag. The setting up of the Rights and Licenses Department at Suhrkamp in the early 1950s, when the founder Peter Suhrkamp was still at the helm, was based on the well-founded supposition that the drawing up of contractual agreements between author and publishing house can only occur in close cooperation between the publisher and the rights department. Implementing the contents of the author's contract is ultimately the responsibility of the publisher and those responsible for the overall publishing programme.

The content of this volume refers first and foremost to the dissemination of literature, non-fiction and academic books but can be applied to all other areas of bookselling too. The explanations are aimed at colleagues working in purchase and sale of rights as well as the editors. They provide guidance for practical use and reveal how the joint success of author and publishing house are inextricably linked to the correct structure and implementation of the author's contract. To a large extent, the work of the publisher, editors and operative departments such as production, sales, advertising and rights and permissions depends on this implementation. Cost-effectiveness and dissemination can be achieved with the cooperation of all those who work in the publishing house, the author, and the national and international audience that both parties attract. I hope that with these explanations I am able to offer assistance to all those who use this reader.

This English edition is the fourth language edition of this practical reader after its publication in

German, Chinese and Arabic. I am very grateful to my publishers Klaus Bramann, Chen Xin, Mustafa Al-Slaiman and Naveen Kishore. A special thanks to the Goethe Institut New Delhi for the translation grant of this edition. This English edition is a revised version of the German. The chapter on digital rights was written by Christoph Hassenzahl, Nora Mercurio, Manuel Quirin and Janika Rüter. We are working in the Rights and Foreign Rights Department at Suhrkamp and I am very grateful for the opportunity to work with a younger generation at the beginning of the digital age in publishing, which is ushering in new conventions for all books in print and electronic form.

1
BUYING RIGHTS

The economic prosperity of a publishing house is very closely linked to the nature of its contracts with its authors. The contractual agreements between the author and the publishing house represent the start of both a 'joint risk' aimed at achieving economic independence for each party and a long-term dialogue with readers. Copyright guarantees the author as the originator of personal rights and rights of use. Personal rights are non-transferable. On the other hand, the author transfers rights of use to the publishing house to ensure his income and the maximum distribution of his works.

> The publishing house shall commit itself
> to producing the work with appropriate
> care, to advertising the work, and to ensure
> the widest distribution among both the
> trade and general public.[1]

The definition of its obligations in the author's
contract forms a fundamental part of the dialogue
between the publishing house and the author. As
the publishing house is given a considerable freedom of legal arrangement, it is called on to pay
attention to the author's wishes. The extent to
which it can take the author's ideas into consideration with regard to the production of a work, the
development of marketing strategies, its distribution in the book trade and its placement across the
various media depends on the nature of the ideas,
their feasibility and the relationship between it and
the author. The success enjoyed by independent
European publishing houses such as Gallimard,
Albin Michel, Feltrinelli, Adelphi, Anagrama,
Suhrkamp and Hanser stems from their ability to
repeatedly redress the balance between the author's
wishes and their own economic considerations, and
to include all the employees of the publishing house
in this interplay, thus motivating them to put in
maximum effort.

In this context, Siegfried Unseld [1924–2002; began to work at Suhrkamp in 1952 and took control of the publishing house when its founder, Peter Suhrkamp, died in 1959] wrote in 1978: 'With regard to the flowing literary communication process there may well have been minor changes to the obligations of a literary publishing house but in principle these are the old ones: to be prepared for the author, for what is new in his work, and to help make it effective.'

1.1
DIRECT DOMESTIC AUTHOR'S CONTRACT

With regard to a long-term relationship between an author and a publishing house, it is imperative that the fundamental elements pertaining to the transfer of rights be laid down in a contract. To this end, the contract is made valid exclusively for the duration of the copyright period, without geographic restrictions and for all editions and print runs.

REQUISITE CONTENTS OF AUTHOR'S CONTRACT

- Duration of the copyright period
- Exclusivity of the rights
- Geographical non-limitation of the rights
- Rights for all editions and print runs

- Effective subsidiary rights at the time of the contract being signed
- Rights for all languages

Mandatory terms of protection based on the Berne Convention and the Universal Copyright Convention differ from country to country with regard to the duration of the copyright period. In Europe, the copyright period has been decided as extending to 70 years following the author's death. Over the past few years, the validity period of publishing contracts has become the subject of discussion and debate between authors and publishing houses. On the one hand, many authors resist contracts that are valid beyond their own death; on the other, there is evidence of increasing influence from literary agents on the relationship between authors and publishing houses. The endurance of the few remaining major independent publishers in Europe and the US is decisively linked to the period of the contract. For the new markets in Asia, Africa and the Middle East it is still not too late to resort to the findings of successful independent publishing houses and to make their authors' contracts valid for as long as possible.

Plans to publish an author's entire body of work require the maximum possible time period. The use of works by Thomas Bernhard, Bertolt Brecht, Hermann Hesse and Rainer Maria Rilke by the publishing houses Suhrkamp and Insel is just one example of how continued economic efforts can only be justified if the publishing house has a very large time period available in which to achieve the desired returns from its economic endeavours in markets at home and abroad, and, moreover, to keep up a constant demand for such works. A 20- to 30-volume edition of an author's collected works, suitably annotated, can only be financed if all rights to the author's entire works are available for a period of time that also applies after his or her death.

Should the author grant the publishing house rights of use for the appropriate COPYRIGHT PERIOD, it is obliged to ensure that the work is available during that time. Publishing houses with a long backlist are aware of the storage and production costs that need to be invested in order to meet the obligations of the contracted period. Should the work no longer be available and the publishing house not be in a position—or not be willing to—reprint within a period of 12 to 18 months after being requested to do so by the author, then the rights of use return to the author.

EXCLUSIVE RIGHTS OF USE provide a publishing house with an opportunity to distribute the work to the exclusion of all other houses.

Use of this principal right is carried out WITHOUT GEOGRAPHICAL RESTRICTION. Granting this right is a prerequisite for the worldwide marketing of publisher's editions and is indispensable in the era of Internet book sales.

Exclusive rights of use to the distribution of publisher's editions without geographical restriction cover all types of editions that the publishing house can offer. The principal editions are: hardback, special hardback, paperback, special paperback, large-print and collectors' editions. If publishing houses have their own book club, audio book club, theatre and media imprint and digital products, then these rights need to be included and mentioned in the contract.

Over the past 10 years, several publishing houses have extended the range of their own use to include aspects that previously featured in the use of subsidiary rights (digitization, new data and audio media, among others). The author has the right to a separate fee for each such use.

Extensive own use on the part of a publishing house leads to parallels with the catalogue of subsidiary rights. For economic reasons, the publishing house will give priority to its own use. It is also obliged to make use of the principal right granted by the author and to reward him or her appropriately.

One of the most important decisions for a publishing house is the strategic weighing-up between own use and third-party use of a work which is protected by a long contract period and which has proved itself successful as a backlist title. In the case of own and third-party use, multiple use can occur either at a later date or concurrently.

Unlike the use of the principal right, the publisher is entitled but not obliged to exploit the subsidiary rights. This is a sensitive issue in the dialogue between publishing house and author: if the publishing house has been unsuccessful in distributing the work in the subsidiary rights segment, it may be accused by the author of inactivity and inability to implement those rights. The publishing house, on the other hand, may claim there was insufficient market demand and be able to prove this.

The subsidiary rights present a catalogue of highly different forms of use in the print and media segment. The circle of licensed partners includes international book publishing houses, the media, film companies, theatres, audio-book publishing houses and digital users.

The right to translate the work into another language has a special position in this catalogue. Once sold, it becomes a principal right.

1.1.1
Contract Subject Matter and Contract Partners

Once a manuscript or its summary has been examined and a decision regarding its position in the publishing programme has been taken, the planning for the own use of a work begins. First, one must determine the contract partner (the author or owner of the copyrights) and the subject matter of the contract (the manner and scope of the work). The greatest possible precision with regard to the integrity of the contract's subject matter is a prerequisite for formulating appropriate remuneration proposals for the author and for the house to make economically sound calculations regarding the future of the work.

In the case of SEVERAL AUTHORS, thought should be given as to whether they are to be given a joint contract or individual contracts governing the same contract subject matter, as is frequently the case with academic works or correspondences. In such cases, a reference to the co-author or authors, with whom a separate author's contract is to be signed, must appear.

Should the author be dead and the publishing house publish a WORK FROM THE ESTATE, then the contract partner is the legal heir—the so-called owner of the copyright. He must be able to prove this through a certificate of inheritance or a certified copy of the author's last will and testament. Should the contract partner be an academic institution, a political association or a media company, it must prove, with the appropriate documentation, its authorship and entitlement to represent the subject matter of the contract.

The SUBJECT MATTER of the contract—the 'Work'—must be stated IN ITS ENTIRETY: this refers not only to the title and subtitle but also to all additions included in the subject matter of the contract such as external articles, illustrations and digital and audiovisual data. If the list of such additional objects of the contract is very long, then it can be included in an additional paragraph or appendix; this paragraph or appendix must be referred to in the subject matter of the contract and is to be thereafter identified as a constituent part of the contract. Should the manuscript not be available in its entirety at the time of the contract being signed, the summary and correspondence with the editors relating to the 'work' may be identified as constituents of the author's contract.

The TITLE can be a provisional or working title or the work's final name: while making a decision about the title, the publishing house must take into account the author's moral rights and choose one preferably in agreement with the author.

The definition of MAXIMUM LENGTH is binding for the author. The publishing house is entitled to withdraw from the contract should the author fail to comply with this condition in such a way that the work, due to its length, nullifies any sensible economic calculation. In the case of literary works, the publishing house must act as it sees fit.

The DATE FOR HANDING IN THE MANUSCRIPT is an indispensable constituent of the author's contract. In the case of literary works, the date on which the manuscript is received is also the date on which the contract is signed.

For literary works, the following applies: should an author's contract be signed on the basis of a summary or a declaration of intent by the author, then the publishing house must have the necessary patience for the author to complete his or her work. Inclusion of the unfinished manuscript in the publishing programme and in sales forecasts is not, in such cases, advisable.

The same is true of standard academic works that are relevant beyond current debates. Here too the author must be given sufficient leeway to complete his or her work. The hand-in date is only approximate with regard to literary and academic works.

This cannot be said of non-literary works based on current topics, or anniversary publications. In such cases, the publishing house must insist on the manuscript being handed in on time, which will in turn determine the length of its production process and its timely publication. The editor must keep in mind both a realistic deadline for the author as well as the timeframes of the publishing house while deciding, in such cases, on an exact hand-in date.

Although legislation in many countries states that the publishing house must begin production as soon as it is in possession of the complete work in printable form, the author can insist on a PUBLICATION DATE being included in his or her contract. However, most contracts signed directly with the author do not include a publication date.

The advance, made on the basis of anticipated sales, already guarantees that the publishing house is doing everything it can to be able to offset this initial investment. The author must, in his or her turn, also adapt to the scope of its publishing programme and grant it—for it is the one bearing the financial risk—discretionary power to decide the best time for the work's publication.

The contract also contains information about THE WORK'S PLACE IN THE PROGRAMME: when the contract is signed, the author knows whether his work is to be published as a hardback or paperback edition, whether it will appear as part of the house's various series or as an individual title in its list. Identifying and stating the work's place in the list is an indication of how the author is positioned in the house's general structure as well as of the sales anticipated with its publication. As such, proof of this should be related to the remuneration.

1.1.2
Print Run, Retail Price, Availability and the Possibility of an Author Withdrawing

The publishing house determines the size of the first, and all subsequent, print runs as well as the retail price. The SIZE OF THE FIRST PRINT RUN is one of the most important decisions to be made by the publishing house prior to the publication of a work. It is a fundamental part of its calculations and a key factor in determining sales. There are various aids (marketing, sales and representatives' estimates) for determining the first print run, and that help reduce the risk although they do not eliminate it entirely. This applies primarily to literary works. The contract can include, in very rare cases, a guaranteed print run for the author. This is not the rule though, as the publishing house must retain the freedom to make a decision on a point which is pivotal to its making a profit or a loss.

The publishing house alone also decides on THE RETAIL PRICE. There is less risk here, however, as the retail price is determined by taking into account the production costs, the remuneration costs, the discounts within the trade and the house's general costs. Fixed retail prices for books in several European countries help calculate, with a large degree of certainty, the income that can be expected from individual titles. Further, the net retail price resulting from the fixed retail price provides a reliable basis for assessing the author's remuneration.

The CONTRACT applies for as long as the work is available. In the most favourable cases, this is for the duration of the copyright period. Should the first edition of the work be unavailable, the author can withdraw from the contract if a fresh print run or a new edition is not produced by that publishing house within a certain period of time. The author can, at any time, check the availability of his work as well as ensure that the publishing house is adhering to the deadlines for subsequent editions or print runs as defined in the contract.

The publishing house is also obliged to inform the author if it is forced to sell his or her book at a reduced retail price during the contract period, due either to dwindling sales or the availability of large stocks. This alters the basis for assessing the author's remuneration and should occur three years after publication at the earliest. If it is not possible to sell the available stock and if the author makes use of his right of withdrawal, then the publishing house has to pulp the remaining stock.

Due to digital printing and other processes that make works permanently available on databases, agreements on the AVAILABILITY of the works are currently in the throes of change. However, technical possibilities in no way alter the responsibility of the publishing house to inform the author whether or not it intends to continue publishing the work in the future. Any attempt to prolong the period of the contract by reprinting the work at the request of the author merely to retain its rights and without any clear purpose in mind with regard to the publishing programme is incompatible with the ethics of the author's contract.

1.1.3
Royalties and Advance Payments

Remuneration for the conferred rights of use of the subject of the contract is its most important constituent for both parties. The economic betterment of both publishing house and author are dependent on negotiations about remuneration and advances. Despite all recommendations and agreements between authors and user parties, the level of the royalty rate for sold copies in relation to the net retail price is a matter for negotiation. (See Appendix A for a suggested royalty scales.)

As a rule, the publishing house offers the author a SLIDING-SCALE ROYALTY related to the number of copies sold. Here it should be examined whether the remuneration can relate solely to the subject matter of the contract or whether additional royalties are also due. If there is a fee framework of 10 per cent for a hardback copy, then all other fees (translation costs, foreign licenses, image rights, etc.) must be deducted. Costs incurred by the author (research, travel, etc.) and billed to the publishing house must be listed separately and, likewise, be deducted from the starting fee.

In the case of texts with a very low print run and works with expensive production processes, the author can be expected to receive no royalty for the first 1,000 copies. Instead, he receives an increased number of free copies. From copy no. 1,001, a sales royalty is in place. Flat-rate remuneration for the first print run and a subsequent sliding-scale royalty is another possibility.

The editorial desks and rights department— who as a rule draw up the contracts—must take care that the sliding-scale royalty negotiated with the author concur with the publishing house's ROYALTY STRUCTURE. There is nothing more counterproductive for a publishing house than inconsistencies in this field. Should the author sign a contract with a publishing house for the first time, he or she has the right to be informed of its royalty structure. If the author is signing a second or third contract, care must be taken that royalty levels are maintained across contracts or, over the years and due to an

increase in the number of available works, even
improved. Authors must be able to rely on the publishing house to bear their interests in mind.

The APPROPRIATE ADVANCE on the expected royalty is a much-discussed part of the contract. It is
also the part over which the views of the publishing
house and those of the author frequently differ. The
level of the advance is geared to the first print run
as anticipated at the time of the contract being
signed, as well as the retail price and the starting
royalty rate. Regarded as a non-returnable guaranteed royalty, the advance payment is set off against
income from book sales only or all earnings.

The publisher or editor submits an offer to the
author about the level of the advance and the
PAYMENT METHOD. If an agreement is reached, the
standard model of 50 per cent payment on signing
of the contract and 50 per cent on appearance of
the work can be varied in several ways. Various
payment methods are conceivable:

- *Single payment* when the contract is signed,
  when the manuscript is handed in or upon
  publication
- *Half* when the manuscript is handed in and
  accepted, and half upon publication

- *One third* when the contract is signed, one third when the manuscript is handed in and the remaining upon publication.

This list can be extended at will. There is no limit to the scope of negotiation between the author and the publishing house with regard to this particular point and the latter is advised to take the author's wishes into consideration at the same time as it bears in mind its own ability to ensure the levels and methods of payment.

These illustrations represent an ideal scenario. In reality, however, things are sometimes different. Extremely high levels of advance have become a recent marketing tool. In this respect, what is most called for is strength and solidarity among publishing houses to resist unrealistic requests.

1.1.4
Subsidiary Rights

The types of subsidiary rights use that should be included in the author's contract depend on various factors:

- What administrative, personnel and economic capacity does the publishing house have to protect the subsidiary rights 'in the best interest of the author'?

- What opportunities do respective national book markets offer for licensing print and non-print rights? As a rule, subsidiary rights granted in authors' contracts at European and US publishing houses encompass a variety of configurations.

CATALOGUE OF SUBSIDIARY RIGHTS

- Translation
- Previews and extracts in newspapers and magazines (first serial and second serial rights)
- Anthology rights
- Book club editions; paperback editions by third parties; newsstand editions; special editions by third parties; abridged versions (print rights)
- Film adaptations; stage performances; lectures (performance rights)
- Radio and TV broadcasting rights (recording rights)
- Audio books/versions; DVDs; MP3s (audio rights)
- E-books (electronic rights)
- Advertising and merchandising rights

- Copyright collecting society

As mentioned earlier, the publishing house is entitled but not obliged to grant subsidiary rights. This interpretation of the law protects the publishing house. At the same time, the author has a right to assume that different types of subsidiary rights use will be realized proactively. Should, for example, the publishing house not have a department of its own that is in a position to offer the film and stage rights for further use, it should pass on this activity to an agency or to the author. The publishing house should also inform the author which subsidiary rights it would like to administer itself and which through an agency. The publishing house must bear in mind that in the case of a sub-agent making use of the sale of subsidiary rights, the author generally forfeits 10 per cent of the royalties thus earned.

The author and the publishing house divide equally the ROYALTIES from the sale of print and electronic subsidiary rights. The author receives 60 per cent of those from media subsidiary rights. Most publishing houses offer the author 60 per cent for translation rights as well. Some houses, who are well known for their special policy regarding authors, grant authors 70 per cent for all non-print and translation rights. For film adaptations, the author's share can amount to even 80 per cent.

The author is able to remove individual rights from the catalogue of subsidiary rights, either because he or she has an opportunity to realize them or because he or she rules out certain uses for the work. This can relate to the audio version, to which not all works are suited, or abridged editions. It can, however, also relate to the translation rights for certain languages; the author may want to pursue those personally.

The publishing house should inform the author that, regardless of the period and the form of use, the granting of subsidiary rights also serves to protect the work from copyright-related encroachments. Further, granting full subsidiary rights that come into effect as soon as the contract is signed enables the publishing house to draw on various synergies for the dissemination of the work.

Prior to granting subsidiary rights, the publishing house should inform the author and, if necessary, await his or her written agreement, even if this is an additional administrative burden in everyday proceedings. Respect for the copyright holder should not be undermined, particularly due to the sensitive issue of subsidiary rights. Acquisition and use of subsidiary rights means offering to disseminate the work across various media and guaranteeing that the work is protected from copyright violations by third parties.

1.1.5
Electronic Rights

For publishing houses, the digital era presents new challenges in terms of author support and control over their work. These challenges can only be met if publishing houses adapt by demonstrating enormous modernization potential.

Authors' contracts must now be extended to cover ELECTRONIC USE. As with printed books, this involves a detailed description of the DIGITAL EDITIONS and trade outlets and formats in which the e-books will appear. The technical aspects must be defined more clearly than in the case of the printed books. Naturally, the biggest question that remains and receives the most attention is that of remuneration: here, international debate is concentrated equally on what share the publishing house and what share the author should receive from sales of e-books. The traditional point of view assumes that the absence of paper/material, printing, storage and distribution costs justifies a higher share for the author. While the continental European version of income division was traditionally based on retail price, the point of reference is shifting—due to the prevalence of Anglo-American standards—to a remuneration basis oriented on net sales. An income division *after* deduction of bookseller discounts leads to significantly less predictable results if, on the one hand, these discounts vary a great deal and, on the other, the booksellers are able to freely determine their pricing for the end customers.

In 2010, two remuneration models apply for the most part:

- 20 or 25 per cent of the net sales revenue are paid to the author; or

- 15–20 per cent of the download price of the e-book, which should not have a price difference of more than 25 per cent with the print edition.

Whether an advance should be paid on these revenues is a matter for negotiation between the author and the publishing house. Both parties are in a so-called start-up phase. Results that are based on experience on the book market will only be available in five years' time.

1.1.6
The Option Clause

The author can grant the publishing house an option on his or her next work. This OPTION CLAUSE is not a constituent of the standard contract, and most European legislation regarding copyright and publishing states that the granting of this option is only valid with an additional payment: as a rule, 5–10 per cent of the advance for the subject matter of the contract. Should there be a further author's contract, the payment made can be credited against the new advance. By granting an option, the author is committed to offering his work first to this publishing house. The publishing house then has four weeks in which to submit an offer to the author. Should it decide against doing so, the author is at liberty to look for a different publishing house. The author keeps the option payment.

The problem with the option clause is not the procedure but the question of its purpose: the trust between a publishing house and an author ought to be such that this arrangement is not necessary. Further, it makes little sense to bind an author to the publishing house by means of one option clause alone if and when he or she would wish to change publishing houses.

1.1.7
Termination of the Author's Contract

The publishing house can TERMINATE THE AUTHOR'S CONTRACT before the work appears if the author does not comply with the hand-in date. In the case of non-fictional books on current topics and for specific occasion (anniversaries, sports events, commemoration days, etc.), late deliveries can jeopardize planned sales programmes. In such a case, the author must return the advance. The publishing house can also terminate the contract should the manuscript reveal qualitative shortcomings. The author is obliged to comply with the house's requests for revisions. Should the result still not meet with its requirements, the contract with the author can be terminated.

1.2
CONTRACTS WITH FOREIGN AUTHORS VIA AN AGENT OR A FOREIGN PUBLISHING HOUSE

Usually the publishing house acquires the rights of use to a foreign author's work via an agency or a foreign publishing house. Unlike the basic prerequisites for maximum own and third-party use for the benefit of both contract partners (rights for the duration of the copyright, without geographic restrictions, for all languages, all editions and print runs and for all subsidiary rights that came into effect at the time the contract was signed), the publishing house has to work with divergent parameters in the case of contracts involving foreign parties. Such contracts are:

- For a limited period
- Restricted to a single language
- Limited to a specific edition
- Offset advances only against sales and for the publication period.

Over the last 20 years, these tendencies have asserted themselves with increasing force. It is difficult to comprehend that contracts with a domestic author and, in some cases, those with a foreign author should differ so greatly from the those signed with an author's agency.

This trend has infected publishing houses too. When they grant translation rights, most of them are unwilling to forego the constituents of the contract mentioned above. Contracts signed with foreign authors until 1980 were generally made out for the duration of the copyright period, providing the Work was in print, in stock and available. Some publishing houses continue with contracts of this nature although they are in the minority. The reasons for this are obvious: the expansion of rights trading throughout the world is stretching many publishing houses to their administrative and logistic limits. Publishing houses with an extensive list of available works handle up to 500 new contracts a year for their authors. Contracts for a limited period may therefore become the norm because it is simpler to declare that the rights are terminated on a specific day than to carefully examine royalty payments or the directory of available works for various markets and editions to see if it is necessary to ask for a return of the rights. There is also an economic aspect: if a contract is prolonged, a refresher advance may be payable.

These are serious consequences, particularly when publishing literary and academic material from abroad, as the publishing house needs far greater economic range and longer time periods for its investments (in translation costs, additional advertising and marketing strategies) to establish a foreign author in its list and across the media.

Other than this, all the sections of the author's contract outlined in 1.1 apply equally in the case of a contract with a foreign author. As such, all that we are concerned with here is clarifying the differences.

CONTRACTS WITH FOREIGN AUTHORS

- Are for a limited period
- Are for a single language, either with or without geographical restrictions
- Are for one edition
- Promise an advance set off against book sales
- Grant restricted subsidiary rights

Contracts with foreign authors are usually signed for the publication of the work in a single language and with a geographically restricted distribution. For languages spoken in several countries and continents, the boundaries of the SALES AREA must be precisely defined. Since 2007, the discussion of sales areas in English- and Spanish-speaking countries has resurfaced due to the advances made by Australian, Indian and Argentinean publishing houses who resist the supremacy of American, English and Spanish publishers in their own sales areas.

If it is not possible for the contract to be valid for the entire copyright period, then it should be VALID for a period of at least 10 years from the date of publication. Shorter periods of validity have an adverse affect on the distribution of the work

and should therefore not be considered. Limited periods of validity can be extended by an additional
clause: that validity is automatically prolonged after
its date of expiry if sales of the work add up to at
least 100 copies per year and if there are at least 100
copies of the work readily available or at the
printer's. This solution has the clear advantage of
the publishing house not having to pay a refresher
advance in the case of the contract being prolonged,
and as such is preferable to all other models.

The contract should include the possibility of
various EDITIONS: the rights for at least two types of
print editions (hardback and paperback) and own
digital use. Should the house not have its own series
of paperbacks, it can arrange for additional use
through a hardback edition. The contracts of an
agent or foreign partner often refer to one type of
edition only, which is why particular attention
should be paid to this point. The house will point
out the various possibilities for its own use, including all forms of print, media and digital use.

The guidelines outlined in **1.1.3** apply here too,
albeit with the major difference that the cost of
translation must be included in the negotiations
determining the level of royalties. If total royalties

of 10 per cent of the net retail price per sold book are available, then the translation costs must be deducted from this figure. In other words, the publishing house should offer starting royalties of 7 per cent for the first print run. Should there be an agreement with the translator for royalties on sales as of a certain print run, this must also be taken into account in the contract negotiations.

Unfortunately, the LEVEL OF ADVANCES on expected royalties has become an instrument of power in international rights trading and its original purpose— of guaranteeing the author royalties on the first print run—has been lost. Further, many agencies have begun paying advances that are considerably higher than the guaranteed fee for the first print run set off against the turnover from book sales. Such astronomical gestures push a publishing house to its limits, endangering its independence and that of its authors. The only response to the inappropriate demands from a handful of agents and publishing houses is increased quality assurance efforts with regard to authors and the handling of works.

The INCLUSION OF SUBSIDIARY RIGHTS in contracts with foreign authors depends on the market. The range of uses extends from one to more than 10 forms in terms of print, media, mechanical and digital reproductions. The house must insist on transferring those subsidiary rights it has classified as indispensable for the economical distribution of the work. Most contracts contain an ADDENDUM stating that subsidiary rights can only be granted following a written agreement from the proprietor. This restriction protects both parties from making wrong decisions in the granting of subsidiary rights, though the original publishing house must rely on the judgement of the contract partner with regard to the authenticity of the licensed partner's offer. The net revenue from the proceeds of subsidiary rights are divided between the original publishing house and the licensee, as a rule 60:40 or 50:50 in favour of the original publishing house.

Depending on the degree of difficulty of the text, the PUBLICATION PERIOD ranges from 12–36 months following the signing of the contract. The publishing house is obliged to commission the translation immediately after acquiring the rights. Should completion of the translation be delayed, the publication period should be sought to be prolonged. In this case many agencies and publishing houses require a renewed payment of the expected royalties. Qualified translations are a prerequisite for the dissemination of a work, and these require time. They also pose a variety of difficulties; hence the publication period should be calculated keeping all this in mind.

Note

1 Suhrkamp Verlag Author's Contract, § 1.2

2
PROTECTING RIGHTS

Fiction and academic works require a publishing programme that is in a position to do editorial and operative justice to the author's work for the duration of the copyright period and to ensure its permanent distribution. For this reason, protecting rights extends beyond work on and with contracts. It is the focal point of all publishing work and embraces all aspects of the area that covers author and publishing house. The preservation and extension of the legal status are decisive for the future of a publishing house and its authors in terms of content, publishing programme and economics.

The author's contract requires its status to be regularly checked by editorial offices and rights departments to ensure it is up to date.

- The period of its validity
- Royalty fees
- Additions, as a result of new programme areas
- Additions, as a result of new types of use
- Converting to a general contract

2.1
THE DIALOGUE WITH THE AUTHOR

What responsibility does the publishing house have to an author who has transferred the rights of his works for the duration of the copyright period? What arrangements are to be made with the heirs following the death of an author? The publisher and the editor are primarily responsible for the relationship with the author. They are able to do this only to the extent that the operative departments of a publishing house relieve them of checking the legal status of the works. Following the appearance of the work, this refers primarily to maintenance of the contract, the backlist and the settlement of royalties.

Ideally, the need to prolong AUTHORS' CONTRACTS WITH LIMITED PERIODS should occur only in the case of foreign authors who are represented by an agent or their original publishing house. The validity period of a contract plays a major role in determining print runs and sales strategies as well as the possible granting of subsidiary rights. In the interest of a long-term relationship with the author, the house should take care early on to prolong expiring contracts and integrate these efforts into its publishing programme.

Should limited contracts be subject to special due diligence because they require frequent amendments, this applies all the more if the author has transferred the rights for the DURATION OF THE COPYRIGHT PERIOD in order to adapt the agreements to current trends. Should the publishing house have introduced new series in its publishing programme or established new imprints, or should new forms of use emerge as a result of new technologies, these changes must be included in the existing contracts in the form of an ADDENDUM. This applies first and foremost to contracts signed prior to the revised version governing new forms of use.

Monitoring of PAYMENT RECEIPTS from book sales is conducted by the accounts and from the sale of subsidiary rights by the royalties account department. In conjunction with the half-yearly or annual royalty payments to authors by the creditors in the royalties bookkeeping department, payment receipts are an important tool in planning the publishing programme and in backlist maintenance. As such, the processing of this information occurs in close cooperation with those responsible in the rights and licensing department, the publisher and the editors. The continual monitoring of payment receipts through sales of own editions and royalty payments from the granting of translation rights and media, electronic and print subsidiary rights is the core responsibility of a rights and licensing department.

An exact account of receipts from book sales of the translation of a work is a prerequisite for estimating the readership reach in foreign markets. In the case of negative figures or sales figures lower than the minimum requirement stipulated in the contract, the original publisher can decide whether to repossess the rights or to encourage the license holder to demonstrate more creativity in its own and third-party use. The consequences resulting from monitoring the foreign editions of a work or its other uses through subsidiary rights form part of the dialogue between the author and the publishing house about the dissemination of his or her work.

MAINTENANCE OF THE BACKLIST and the processing of existing rights for new publications are responsibilities of the publisher and the editors that have a major influence on the economic success of a publishing house and its authors. Monitoring the availability of the works is primarily the responsibility of the editors and the programme managers in close cooperation with sales, production and rights and licensing departments. The aim must be to have at least one edition available of each of the author's works. This can only be achieved if the publishing house has sufficient planning time. Should the contract be limited, all reproductions included in the author's contract must be produced within a predetermined period; this restricts the number of possible reproductions and editions, which puts the author at a disadvantage.

In this chapter, it should be assumed that the publishing house has the rights to a work for as long as it is available. A publishing house's most important responsibility is to enter into a lifelong dialogue with the author regarding its publishing intentions. In contrast to the pressure to succeed on the publication of a new manuscript, a publishing house can approach the maintenance of its backlist with calm strategy. Suggestions by the publishing house are presented to the author, and his wishes and reservations taken into account.

MAINTENANCE OF THE BACKLIST

- *Available editions.* How many editions of a single work can a publishing house keep available in various price categories? Is it possible to guarantee parallel hardback, paperback, collectors' editions and e-books?
- *Possibility of integration in series.* Is the work suitable for a specific series (world literature, poetry, biographies, textbooks, anthologies)?
- *New print runs.* Can the work be re-released to mark specific occasions (author's birthday, anniversaries relating to the contents, historic events, cultural events, etc.)?
- *Promotional editions.* Is the work suitable for market-oriented promotions such as holiday reading, seasonal books, educational journeys, public holidays, lifestyle and *zeitgeist*?
- *Subsidiary rights exploitation.* In addition to own rights use, can the subsidiary rights be used either simultaneously or at a later date?

The position afforded to a title in the overall publishing programme and the publishing schedule determine the reception of the individual and collected works of an author. To allow oneself to be guided by market trends in these considerations—which, in terms of consumer patterns, are difficult to estimate and verify—is wrong. The publishing house's aim must be to publish literature and important works in the humanities and natural sciences in such a way that they withstand, accompany and influence social change.

The translation of an author's work into a foreign language enjoys a special status in the relationship between author and publisher. Translations and the author's subsequent appearances in other countries can boost his professional literary career and, in an ideal scenario, make him internationally renowned. The cross-border impact of literature and academic work can only come to full fruition on the basis of qualified translations. Granting these rights to the correct publishing partner abroad is the responsibility of the publishing house. Authors should support these efforts accordingly. As such, authors should recognize that, in addition to the publisher who publishes their original editions, they have other publishing houses abroad with which they should maintain contact.

What is decisive for his relationship with the foreign publisher applies all the more to his relationship with translators. Many authors work very closely with their translators and not infrequently, this relationship spans a lifetime. Insofar as it is possible, the publishing house is advised to check the quality of translations and, where necessary, demand that the foreign publishing house have them revised and reworked. Translations of works that are more than 30 years old need to be commissioned afresh. It is the responsibility of the publishing house to insist upon a new translation that is suited to the current reception of the work.

In addition to the possibilities offered by its print editions, a work can be investigated for FURTHER USES. These primarily involve:

- Audio books
- Readings or dramatizations on radio or TV and recordings of them on CDs/DVDs
- E-books, for offline or online consumption
- Screen adaptations

The publishing house will either integrate these forms of reproduction into its own programme or license them out to a third party. In such cases, agreement with the author is particularly important, especially if the new medium requires changes be made to the original work. The choice of license partner can also only be made in close collaboration with the author. The original publishing house's standards must be maintained across all other uses. The author should have a say in the external form of the licensed version of his or her work, as well as in changes to its title and content.

Should, over an extended period of time, more than 10 works by a particular author have appeared in a publishing house and still be available, and should the collaboration have proved beneficial for both parties economically and conceptually, it is meaningful to sign a GENERAL CONTRACT for all previously published works and those that will appear during the author's lifetime. Arrangements for publications from the estate require a separate agreement within such a general contract, or an addendum. The general contract must be concluded for the duration of the copyright period. It must also include all rights applicable at this point in time so as to cover the various forms of reproduction in the company's own programme as well as those made possible by the subsidiary rights granted.

The financial reward an author can expect from a general contract is a matter for negotiation between him or her and the publisher. This can take the form of a yearly or monthly advance payment on all the expected royalties or a fixed minimum advance when a new manuscript is handed in. A contract such as this ensures the author's financial future and commits the publishing house to the utmost care and maintenance of the work that has already appeared or that will appear in the future.

The list of responsibilities necessary for the maintenance of works must be adapted to new trends in society and book markets. Only through a dialogue with its authors can the publishing house be certain that they accept its plans for its publishing programme and that they are prepared to take full advantage of its domestic and international network in conjunction with their own. The publisher's intuition applies to the publication of an individual work in relation to the entire work. The real art lies in the placement and promotion of a collective body of work within a larger publishing programme.

2.2
MAINTENANCE OF THE WORK
FOLLOWING THE AUTHOR'S DEATH

Upon the author's death, the copyrights (personal rights and rights of use) are transferred to an heir. Collaboration with regard to the maintenance of the work subsequently occurs between the publishing house and the heir. These can be the author's spouse, children, siblings, relatives or an institution.

The administration of the royalties and editorial responsibility for the work need not be handled by a single entity. The publishing house frequently transfers royalties to the natural heirs and conducts the dialogue regarding the maintenance of the work and the editorial agenda of the estate with an organization. This occurs if the heirs consider themselves unable to tend to the deceased's literary or academic work or if there are no natural heirs to take on this responsibility. As far as the publishing house is concerned, it is in every respect most practical if the responsibility for the work rests with a single party. The example of Thomas Bernhard serves to illustrate the options a legacy of this nature can involve and exemplifies how the heir, in this case the author's brother, assumed the responsibility and the steps he took in collaboration with the publishing house to protect his brother's work.

Following the death of Thomas Bernhard on 12 February 1989, the copyrights were transferred to the author's brother, Dr Peter Fabjan. The latter had been familiar with his brother's daily routine and intentions for decades. With regard to the role set out for him in Bernhard's last will and testament, he stated in an interview conducted in the Thomas Bernhard Archive on 24 November 2006: 'My first intention was to follow his wishes to the letter, but it soon turned out that this was completely undermined by reality. From the very outset, all the conditions stated in the will could only be realized in a modified form. I quickly realized that, as had sometimes been the case previously, Thomas had asked for the impossible. He thought big.' The estate administration, founded in 1989 by Fabjan, possesses and maintains the real estate (three farming properties and an apartment in Gmunden) and takes care of all contact with publishing houses, theatres, artists, media and authorities. Fabjan channels a proportion of the royalties and commissions to which he and his sister Susanne Kuhn are entitled to as heirs into financing the three other institutions: the Private Trust, the Thomas Bernhard Archive and the International Thomas Bernhard Society. Of the country properties, the main residence in

Obernthal near Ohlsdorf (in Upper Austria) consumes the lion's share of the finances. The Vierkanthof is open to the public as a memorial; every July and August, it is the venue for readings and theatre events.

On 13 July 1998, Fabjan founded the Thomas Bernhard Private Trust based in Vienna. In accordance with his last will and testament, the Trust represents Bernhard's interests in Austria as well as other countries. As such, the work and the name of the author are protected by a foundation: in other words, in addition to the copyright protection guaranteed by a publishing house, the work is also represented by an institution. The Private Trust sees itself as the sole representative of Bernhard's interests against state intrusion and acquisitions. This way, the heir ensures Bernhard's work the independence essential for the dialogue with all those who have an interest in it. In 1997, in agreement with Federal Chancellor Klima and Cultural Minister Scholten (as representatives of the Federal President and the Republic), Fabjan arranged for the estate and the holdings of Bernhard's work to be transferred to the National Library in Vienna on the expiry of its copyright period in 2059. In return, the state of Austria makes an annual contribution to the Private Trust. The latter coordinates collaboration between the Thomas Bernhard Archive, the International Thomas Bernhard Society based in Vienna, Weimar and Udine, and the Nachlassverwaltung GmbH (Administration of the Estate) in Gmunden. It promotes collaboration with translators as well as theatres and media abroad, thereby establishing a focal point in the network relating to the author and his entire legacy.

'My star will shine. I will return from abroad,' Bernhard said in an interview with Krista Fleischmann, in the light of his conflicts with Austrian politics during his lifetime. Bernhard's works have now been translated into 45 languages and his plays have been performed in theatres through the world. The number of translations Suhrkamp licenses every year is still rising. In order to ascertain the reception enjoyed by the work, Fabjan founded the International Thomas Bernhard Society in 1999, which defines its purpose as follows:

> The International Thomas Bernhard Society sees itself as an international forum for the exchange of information and the provision of contacts to build a network that

links the realms of theater, research, and media with regard to works addressing the creative output of Thomas Bernhard. The Society makes accessible the results of the work performed by the Trust and the Archive and establishes an information platform for all those interested in the life and work of Thomas Bernhard.

For Suhrkamp and Insel, as owners of the rights of Bernhard's works, this structure is ideal. Regarding issues concerning the maintenance of the work and posthumous publications, the publishing house is able to engage both the estate administration and the Private Trust. The publishing house plans all new editions of previously published works, and those from the estate, in close collaboration with Fabjan and the Thomas Bernhard Archive. The 22-volume edition, edited by Wendelin Schmidt-Dengler and Martin Huber, would have been inconceivable without the close collaboration between Raimund Fellinger (the Bernhard editor and chief editor of Suhrkamp), the Archive and the Private Trust.

The institutions and trusts (estate administration, Private Trust, Archive and International Thomas

Bernhard Society) that Fabjan set up in this case to protect Bernhard's work ensure the maximum implementation of what the administrator of an estate can do to protect the rights and work of an author. This implementation is in turn a prerequisite for the publishing house to maintain the work in a manner faithful to the author's wishes.

Whereas in the case of Bernhard the focus is on editions of his complete works, single editions and reproductions of his plays, with other authors it also extends to posthumous publications: Theodor W. Adorno, Paul Celan and Hermann Hesse are prime examples. Posthumous publications also require close collaboration between the heirs, the publisher and the relevant editor. The maintenance of an author's work and estate following his death extends the role of the editor to that of an academic. The finances involved can, in most cases, only be raised through the cooperation of the publishing house and the heirs and is not possible without the help of trusts and university establishments.

Due to the variety of tasks it entails, the diversity of clients and the domestic and foreign economic opportunities it offers, the sale of subsidiary rights is an area of business that requires strategic planning.

3.1
SELLING TRANSLATION RIGHTS

The symbiosis between cultural-political aspects and economic efforts and earnings when a work is translated is much more than in any other area of the reproduction of cultural assets. Of the 30–40 per cent of the remaining income following deduction of the author's share from translation revenues, the publishing house must reinvest a major proportion to

make the author known in the relevant market. To
this end, the publishing house serves as a cultural
navigator, diplomat, mediator, market strategist,
and salesperson all in one. There is scarcely a more
distinguished assignment in the book trade than
conveying works of world literature, the humanities, natural sciences, children's and art books into
other languages and cultures.

With the translation of his or her works into
other languages, an author's impact increases considerably, especially with regard to the geographical
reach of his reception by readers, the media, the
book trade and at universities abroad. An author's
economics improve due to earnings from royalties
from the sale of translations which are supple-
mented every now and then by invitations from and
readings in various countries.

Making an author known above and beyond the
national or same-language market is a task that
emerges from the granting of subsidiary rights use.
This task can only be achieved with a comprehensive knowledge of the international book trade. The
first step in the dissemination of literature and academic works involves selecting the publishing house
that comes into question for the translation.

CRITERIA FOR SELECTING FOREIGN PUBLISHING HOUSES

- How extensive is its list of available works?
- Which national and international authors does it publish?
- Which works by authors contracted to your publishing house has it already translated?
- Do your author's works fit in with its general list?
- Is your author's work supported by a corresponding thematic scope in the foreign publisher's list?
- Who is the prospective translator?
- Which editor will oversee the project?
- Is the foreign publishing house prepared to carefully check and, if necessary, revise the translation?
- What sales and marketing capacity does the foreign publishing house have?

These questions need to be clarified before actual negotiations begin. The aim must be for all license partners to get to know each other so well that, at some point, questions such as these appear super-fluous. In this respect, publishing houses targeting companies specializing in textbooks, children's books and specialist publications have an easier time than a literary or academic publishing house. Experience shows that the latter requires at least 10–20 years to acquire translation contracts for its contemporary authors. Below are two examples relating to the reception and dissemination of works by Jürgen Habermas and Walter Benjamin.

1. In 1996, a young Chinese academic named Cao Weidong entered the Rights and Licenses department at Suhrkamp. He explained that he was one of Jürgen Habermas' students and that he wanted to help make the works of his teacher known in China. With his Chinese colleagues, he wanted to translate *Strukturwandel der Öffentlichkeit* (The Structural Transformation of the Public Sphere), *Nachmetaphysisches Denken* (Postmetaphysical Thinking) and *Philosophischer Diskurs der Moderne* (The Philosophical Discourse of Modernity), as well as some other works by the German philosopher and, where necessary, oversee his colleagues' translations. In 1998, a day before the Frankfurt Book Fair, a 15-man delegation of Chinese publishers visited Suhrkamp. Chen Xin (Director, Century Publishing Group, Shanghai) enquired whether the translation rights to the works of Jürgen Habermas were

available. In a unique form of cooperation between Jürgen Habermas, Cao Weidong, Chen Xin, the author's colleagues at Beijing University and the Chinese Academy of Social Sciences (CASS), the Goethe Institut, the Frankfurt Book Fair, the *Buchhandelsinformationszentrum* (Book Trade Information Centre) in Beijing, and Suhrkamp, licensing partners were located and an initial 10 translation contracts were signed. *Strukturwandel der Öffentlichkeit* (1999*), Nachmetaphysisches Denken* (1999*)* and *Philosophischer Diskurs der Moderne* (2001) appeared in translation by Cao Weidong. By 2006, more than 20 works by Habermas had appeared in China and, following publication, emerged as the long-sellers they already were in other countries.

2. Between 1998 and 2006, over 60 years after Walter Benjamin's death, the best, most carefully edited Benjamin edition in several volumes was published by Harvard University Press. Since the appearance of the first volume, Lindsay Waters, the Benjamin editor, published several secondary reproductions of texts from the complete works in themed editions which attracted the attention of the media in the US. In 2006, more or less simul-

taneously, the first translations of *Passagenwerk*
appeared in Brazilian (Editora UFMG), Korean
(Saemulgyul) and Polish (Wydawnictwo Literackie)
in their respective countries.

These two examples demonstrate that a publishing
house can only economically justify international
endeavours if the author has granted it the main as
well as the subsidiary rights for the duration of the
copyright period. This is an important criterion and
should always be borne in mind when acquiring
rights.

3.1.1
Market and Sector Knowledge

Even in the age of digital communication, personal
contact with the foreign publisher and the foreign
editor is of the utmost importance for the rights
seller and the various INTERNATIONAL BOOK FAIRS
provide a platform for such encounters.

The Frankfurt Book Fair is one of the oldest in
the world (first officially mentioned in 1454 though
some sources date it to the time before Johannes
Gutenberg), and has the most exhibitors even
though it now faces competition from the fair in
London organized by Reed Elsevier. As yet, the

different character of the two fairs has ensured
major international popularity for both locations.
Whereas in London, concentration is focused for
three days on licensing, the Frankfurt fair, with its
development over the course of time and its importance, offers the international book sector greater
scope for intellectual and cultural exchange.

Besides Frankfurt and London, the decision on
which fairs need to be attended in order to close the
best deals for one's authors depends on the profile
and the financial resources of each individual publishing house. As such, publishing houses specializing in children's books attend the International
Children's Book Fair in Bologna, whereas those interested in licensing deals for Eastern European literature visit the fairs in Warsaw and Moscow.

Apart from book fairs, there are numerous other
opportunities for trading and exchanging rights: sem-
inars, colloquia, presentation tours, literature bien-
nials such as that organized by the Frankfurt
Literaturhaus and the extremely valuable 'fellowships'
of, among others, the book fairs in Jerusalem, Frankfurt and Turin. It cannot be overemphasized that any
opportunity that arises and that additionally relieves
the publishing house of financial burden ought to

be used to extend one's own market knowledge and promote discussion of its authors.

The FRANKFURT BOOK FAIR, a private company owned by *Börsenverein des deutschen Buchhandels* (German Publishers and Booksellers Association) supports the efforts made by German publishing houses in an exemplary manner. It organizes joint stands at international book fairs and assists the publishing houses with book trade information centers in Beijing, Warsaw, Bucharest, New Delhi and New York. Institutions of this kind also exist in other countries, providing confirmation that as culturally relevant as books may be, they cannot be perpetuated by a free-market economy alone but require continual cultural and political support, which must not, however, become mixed up in negotiations between publishing houses.

Attending book fairs and other events is an important component in acquiring detailed market and sector knowledge. Regularly reading publishing houses' programmes and visiting their websites is a further prerequisite. Given the scope of these tasks, publishing houses, in which the sale of translation rights represents an above-average share of revenue from subsidiary rights, have begun training individual employees in rights trading departments to specialize in certain markets. Nobody should be put off by the fact that it takes years to acquire this information.

In addition to the direct acquisition of knowledge through the Internet, previews and advertising, it is helpful to read the relevant press and trade journals, inasmuch as language barriers allow, or to fall back on existing English press associations. As a rule, the research and reading mentioned are not possible in the scope of everyday work in a rights and licensing department: one has to invest one's own private time in this further training.

The Frankfurt Book Fair's annual RIGHTS DIRECTORS MEETING, held shortly before the fair opens, provides another good opportunity for expanding one's market knowledge. Anybody unable to attend should obtain the associated documentation.

3.1.2
Intermediaries

The number of professional intermediaries working for the dissemination of literature and academic works is large. A difference should be made between professional intermediaries and those promoting translations in the frame of cultural-political work. In order to achieve the goal of realizing the worldwide dissemination of its authors, a publishing house will, after in-depth examination, decide whom to include in this intermediary process. It must weigh up who is truly prepared to act in the interest of the copyright owner and the owner of the rights of use, and who is primarily pursuing his own cultural or financial goals.

INTERMEDIARIES
IN THE WORLDWIDE LICENSING NETWORK

- Professional intermediaries
- Translators
- Agents
- Scouts
- Intermediaries with a cultural brief
- Cultural institutions, such as the Goethe Instituts
- Universities
- Trusts

TRANSLATORS of German literature and academic works are important partners for rights traders. Many authors work closely and over an extended period of time with the same translators. They have the quality of the translations to thank for their impact abroad, after all. Even though the foreign publishing house chooses the translator, the author's wish for a certain translator must be stipulated in the licensing contract. Insofar as the author does not wish to do so personally, it is courteous to inform translators about their authors' new works and plans.

The translators are an intermediary par excellence. Far beyond their financial interest in the realization of the translation, they are often the only persons promoting the granting of the translation rights at a time when nobody in the publishing houses has yet been made aware of the author in question. Without the selfless efforts of translators many literary works would never have caught the attention of an international readership.

In Europe over the past decades, the fine balance between the art of translating and intermediacy has been increasingly honoured and reflected in prices that acknowledge the achievement of the translation as well as the intermediary role of the translator. This is not the case in all countries: in the US, where there is outstanding quality in the field of translation, insufficient notice is taken by the publishing industry of the American Literary Translators Association which, in November 2007, celebrated its thirtieth anniversary in Dallas.

Whenever possible, the publishing house should sign all contracts directly and not through an agency. In reality, most publishing houses currently work with agencies in various markets. In order to be financially successful, an agency will represent not just one publishing house from a given country but, as a rule, 10–30. The principle of selection that this type of representation entails is inevitably a disadvantage to the individual author and needs to be compensated for by the original publishing house. It is impossible for the agency to guarantee the same level of commitment to all authors, and it focuses primarily on bestseller lists, sales figures and media response. However, the publishing house must not relinquish overall control of further use of the works: even though the agency might well be an important intermediary, it is no substitute for discussions between the publisher, the editors and the respective author.

Through contract administration and maintenance of the backlist, an AGENCY or a SUB-AGENT provides an important form of relief for the original publishing house: it informs the owner about contracts that are about to expire and proposes the terms for their extension. It assists the publishing house in monitoring royalties received and advances paid. A tie to an agent or a sub-agent can be exclusive: in a given country, all contracts and payments pass through it exclusively. Or it can be non-exclusive: the publishing house concludes signs directly or via the agency. This works smoothly in smaller countries; but in larger, financially strong markets, the publishing house must weigh up whether to work independently without an agency or with an exclusive agent.

The LITERARY SCOUT, unlike an agent, works exclusively for a publishing house in a particular market and is also an important discussion partner for all other publishing houses. The sales information given to a scout can provide a high degree of efficiency: if it succeeds in convincing him of the quality and marketability of a title, several translation licenses can be granted through a single business partner. It is only natural that the programmes of those houses that work with the same scout are similar; appropriate to the requirements of his task, he has a clear signature in terms of programme. In many cases, the publishing house with which the first deal was made takes on the role of scout itself.

The publisher that has acquired a foreign title will attempt to exercise his options with fellow publishers in other countries both out of conviction and for strategic reasons; his own plans with regard to the translation, but primarily to the production process and sales and marketing strategies, can then be coordinated with other publishing houses. Jointly planned strategies reduce risk.

In addition to professional intermediaries for literary and academic works abroad there is also the previously mentioned array of cultural and political organizations. Over the past few years, collaboration between the GOETHE INSTITUTS and the publishing sector has significantly improved and intensified, not least of all because one of the most important institutions for the translation of German literature and academic work into foreign languages, the *Übersetzungsförderung* (Translation Grant Programme) has been affiliated to the Goethe Institut in Munich. Whereas in addition to providing language tuition, the institutes are responsible for promoting a wide cultural palette from literature, art and music to theatre, the promotion of translation applies exclusively to literature, academic and children's books and intellectual non-fiction. Despite criticism of too-scant state funding in view of the global market, the importance of this form of subsidy cannot be overemphasized.

The addition of private means to state subsidies from trust funds is indeed helpful but should not play a role in negotiations between publishing houses. The *Börsenverein,* the Federal Foreign Ministry and the Fritz Thyssen Trust enjoyed great success with its new, very effective initiative for subsidizing the translation of academic texts into English.

3.1.3
Strategies

Every copyright owner can assume that his work could also be of interest in other countries. The groundwork involved in selling rights abroad is obvious at first sight: books and material, information, options, offers and the signing of a contract are all indispensable elements. By means of a few examples, I would like to illustrate the additional criteria that the license seller should bear in mind and what preliminary work needs to be performed to close the desired deal.

STEPS IN THE SALE OF TRANSLATION RIGHTS

• *Prior to publication of the work*

(a) A thorough reading of the work as soon as the first proof is available.

(b) Discussion with the editor and the author and expectations relating to its dissemination.

(c) Assessment of whether, prior to publication, a small circle of foreign publishers and agents, with whom one works exclusively, should be sent publicity or advance copies.

(d) Offer the front list or advertising copy in English on the rights website.

(e) The foreign rights catalogue must contain a summary of the work's contents, a biography and bibliography of the author, a copy of the cover, press articles, a photo of the author and a list of the previously granted translation licenses.

(f) Prior to upcoming book fairs, the catalogue must be sent in PDF format to partner publishing houses abroad.

- *On publication of the work*

    (a) Free copies to be despatched to all publishing houses whose interest one would like to raise and to all agents who work with the publishing house.

    (b) Despatch of important reviews to these publishing houses and agents, with the book or separately, depending on the date of publication.

(c) Translation of important excerpts into the relevant language, preferably English, to be sent to the publishing houses and agents.

(d) Publishing houses and agents to be informed of current sales figures and reprints.

- *Four weeks after publication of the work*

  (a) Conduct first appraisal of despatches prior to and concurrent with publication.

  (b) Telephone contact with clients: relay information about the author and the work's success (bestseller lists, literature prizes, etc.).

- *Following receipt of the first offer*

  (a) Inform other publishing houses that are potential license partners in the same country about the first offer.

  (b) Set a deadline by which all offers must have been received and inform potential contract partners of it.

  (c) Make a decision with regard to the sale based on the programme range, level of the offer and the quality of the foreign publishing house's translators.

(d) The foreign publishing house's further commitment is more important than the level of its advance payment.

- *Signing of the contract*

   (a) Once it has been signed, the contract and working copies should be sent to the foreign publishing house as swiftly as possible.

   (b) All other publishing houses and agents contacted are to be informed via the website, by e-mail or verbally of the first signing, which is known to be the most difficult.

- *During the first 12 months following the appearance of the work*

   (a) Identify countries with geographical, linguistic or historical ties with the publishing house who signed the first contract.

   (b) Provide new press reviews and sales figures.

   (c) Determine in discussions with the foreign editors where there is potential for further contracts.

   (d) In the case of rejection, urge the potential license partner to state why. The most common explanation of 'It doesn't really fit in with our programmes' should be elucidated.

(e) If there is a close relationship with the foreign publisher, request expert opinions in order to be able to better appraise the author's image among foreign readers.

The key to being a rights dealer is to acquire such knowledge of the market and the sector in general that one can develop a well-founded, differentiated opinion on which publishing house best suits an author and his works. Decisions made solely on the basis of the level of the advance or best offer reduces strategic action to a purely financial aspect, whereas other criteria (programme position, quality of the translation, etc.) are of greater importance for an author's longevity. The foreign editors who acquire translation rights have their work cut out with the international production of new releases every year. A manner of dealing with offers that lessens the foreign editor's workload by forwarding not just a copy of the work, which as a rule is then passed on to an expert, but also specimen translations, reviews and information about the author, is a prerequisite for that most decisive of working tools: personal contact with the foreign publisher and editor.

A work failing to sell in the first 12 months after publication is no reason to cease one's efforts. With regard to literary and academic works, long-term concepts are necessary and it often takes decades for an author to become established beyond the borders of his own country.

Should an author's works already be available in translation, the general rule is that the publishing house which translated the first book has first refusal for the second work or all others, even if this was not a constituent of the contract (option clause). Cases in which either the author or the publishing house was dissatisfied with the license partner or had objections with regard to the usage of translation rights are an exception to the rule. For authors whose work has already been translated into several languages, the number of foreign publishers should be constantly increased. In so doing, one can and indeed should not only refer to the history of the author's reception at home but also fall back on the experiences of other publishing houses for further possible sales. Reviews, opinions and author interviews in the foreign media also serve to help acquire further contracts.

3.2
USE OF PRINT SUBSIDIARY RIGHTS
IN THE DOMESTIC MARKET

This refers to classic subsidiary rights, the sale of which has a different character from the granting of translation rights. Licensing contracts are concluded neither for the duration of the copyright period nor are they exclusive as a rule. In the use of subsidiary rights, own use takes precedence over third-party use. In other words, any use of the work that can be carried out by the publishing house itself should not, or only after thorough examination, be licensed out individually. This applies not only to print rights (paperbacks and special editions in particular) but also to audio reproduction rights and electronic rights, provided that corresponding forms of publication are available on own labels. As a rule, recording, dramatization and press rights require collaboration with a media partner.

The granting of subsidiary rights is financially profitable, reaches readers in other fields and assists the author's dissemination. It must not, however, be to the detriment of sales of the original edition. For this reason, subsidiary rights that involve the licensee serving DIFFERENT MARKETS from the original publishing house are the most lucrative, as in the case of a book club and many paperback editions. As such, the granting of a licensed edition can also be the result of a sales-related decision. Using a few examples of print subsidiary rights and on the basis of the opportunities that arise from alternating between own and third-party use, I would like to illustrate how subsidiary rights can be used appropriately as a form of author retention and work maintenance.

3.2.1
Paperback Editions

If the publishing house has no paperback programme of its own, the sale of paperback rights forms an easily calculable proportion of annual sales. The granting of a license is based on the author list, the potential license partner's range of themes, its sales and marketing operations and its fee. Here too, the rights seller's duties include the strategic offering of subsidiary rights, targeted planning and a policy with regard to the author that includes a contract with a paperback publisher. The advance should reflect anticipated royalties from the first print run. The contract should run for five to seven years following the appearance of the licensed edition. Given the diversity of its series and its tar-

get group orientation, the paperback market is easy
to observe; demand determines the license market.

IMPORTANT CONSTITUENTS
OF A PAPERBACK LICENSING CONTRACT

- Publication period
- Sliding-scale royalties
- Duration of validity
- Clearance period on expiry of the duration
- Retail price of the paperback edition

Wrong decisions with regard to the publication period and the retail price of the foreign paperback
edition have many repercussions. Should, for example, publication of the paperback occur too early,
and should unit sales figures for the hardback rise
again as a result of a review, a literary prize, a TV
programme, etc., the licensor can miss out on considerable turnover because the paperback publisher
will also pick up on the 'media event' in its advertising campaign for the title. This is a risk factor that
is difficult to predict; therefore, the length of time
between the appearance of a hardback and a paperback edition should be at least 12 months. In the
case of titles that have the aforementioned potential, even 24–36 months.

One alternative for a publishing house with no paperback programme of its own is the commitment as a partner to a paperback publisher which is then given the first option. This model likewise enables reliable sales planning. If the partner publishing house does not exercise the first option, the rest of the market is waiting on the sidelines. Partnerships can also be transferred to print subsidiary rights.

If the licensor has its own PAPERBACK SERIES, it will only very rarely grant licenses to third-party publishing houses. Exceptions are long-sellers that allow third and fourth print runs, reproductions in paperback without having an adverse effect on sales of the original version and licenses for specific sales drives of other paperback publishing houses. In such cases, attention should be paid to a short running time and an even shorter period in which to sell off all stock. The retail price must not undercut the price of the in-house edition and the layout and blurb must correspond to the standard of in-house editions. The licensor's control function must be contained in the licensing contract.

3.2.2
Book Club Editions

Book clubs and book sales clubs are no longer as significant as they were in Europe in the 1920s and, particularly in Germany, in the 1950s. For the most part, this is due to the fact that there is no longer any obligation to buy a product every year or quarter. Since the 1980s, it has been possible to buy good-value hardbacks at cut-price outlets and now, as-good-as-new used books through Internet platforms such as Amazon and eBay. Because the book market is also responding increasingly quickly to new titles and readers are unwilling to wait for a new publication even at a reduced price, membership figures for book clubs are dwindling.

The book club sales channel works on the basis of the membership principle. Book club editions can only be offered to members who have committed themselves to making one or several purchases a year at prices lower than the original. The Potsdam Protocol lists three additional criteria for guaranteed prices for book clubs, namely:

- *The date of appearance*: at a later date than the trade edition, at least four months in the case of a new title.

- *The price*: as a rule this is 20 per cent lower than the trade price.
- *The layout*: this must differ from that of the trade edition.

Over the past few years, the clubs' print run policy, and consequently the level of advances, has diminished considerably: many book clubs are increasingly complementing their turnover with non-print products.

3.2.3
Special Editions

The decline in book club business over the past 10 years has been compensated with a line of business that has existed for a long time in Latin and Anglo-Saxon countries but has only recently emerged in Germany and Central and Eastern European countries: 'newsstand' editions that are bought with magazines and newspapers and also known as 'newspaper' or 'magazine' editions. This line of business, originally intended to compensate for the dramatic fall in sales, has been such a success for several newspaper publishers and media companies that it has developed from a sideline into a new publishing programme. It has, in some cases, even led to the formation of new companies within a publishing group.

The first major drive of this type in Germany by the *Süddeutsche Zeitung* in 2004 precipitated a discussion in the book trade as to the extent to which a hardback in paperback format costing € 4.90 was harmful to sales in the paperback book market in general: the results were evaluated very differently. As the licensor, publishing houses must examine whether activities such as these, which may necessitate a third, large print run, damage sales from its own production. The contracts are valid for 12 to 18 months at most and hence do justice to the promotional character of the license. The royalties are based on the layout and the retail price of the packaged edition: 8–10 per cent for a hardback special edition and 6–8 per cent for a paperback special edition. In some cases, the large print runs can mean large advances, due when the contract is signed. The newspaper publisher bears the risk for this.

The cover design, blurb and advertising are subject to control by the licensor. At the moment, it is difficult to predict the extent to which these licenses will establish themselves in Germany and other countries or whether they have already peaked economically.

3.2.4
Own Print versus Licensed Edition

One of the most interesting aspects of the use of subsidiary rights in the domestic market is the strategic switch between own print and license editions. Whether or not one concludes a licensing contract depends on an estimation of the extent to which it could damage sales from own editions. For this reason, the rights seller should not conduct business in the domestic market without having previously spoken to the executive editors. Should they have objections, the rights seller is obliged to protect its own exploitation and come up with a different solution for market demand. There is always a fine balancing act between the licensee's request, the rights seller's wish to generate sales and the necessarily rigid stance of the sales department, which works under the premise of drumming up turnover with the company's editions.

Before a PAPERBACK LICENCE is granted, the following questions should be taken into account:

- How many copies of the work in question has the publishing house sold over the past three years?

- Have annual sales been declining?

- Is there an anniversary relating to the author or the title approaching?
- Which editions of the same title are already available in the publishing programme?
- How long is the duration of the Author's contract?

If the author's contract has been negotiated for the duration of the copyright period, there is nothing standing in the way of a limited license. This should be non-exclusive, the retail price should not undercut that of the company's own edition and the duration should be two years at most. The publishing house can then consider whether to temporarily withdraw its own paperback edition from the market for the duration of the license and then include it in its programme again. Top-selling titles in one's own programme are not suitable for licensing.

With regard to book club, kiosk, and special editions in the hardback segment, additional aspects should also be taken into consideration:

- Is the requested title available in the own paperback programme?
- How large is the price difference between the own paperback edition and the licensed hardcover edition?

In addition to being used in a publishing house's own programme, mostly bestsellers from the backlist are suitable for multiple licensing in various main and subsidiary markets. In such cases, the clear delineation of market segments, layouts and pricing must be discussed with executive editors and licensors so as to avoid the editions competing with each other. In this respect, the limitation of the contract in terms of geography and time is all the more necessary.

3.3
ADMINISTRATION

Publishing houses that, on account of the nature of their authors' contracts, are authorized to conclude a large number of contracts domestically and abroad require a computerized database to check all relevant contract data, at best on a daily basis.

CHECKING THE CONTRACT DATA FOR

- The name of the contract partner
- The title of the work
- The date of the contract
- The publication period
- The method of advance payment
- The complimentary copies

- The royalties/invoicing
- For the date of the contract's termination
- The clauses of the contract's prolongation

The same applies to the ADDRESS FILE. Each use involves a different circle of clients. With regard to print rights alone, it includes between 2,000 and 4,000 addresses at home and abroad. The files must be maintained and updated every month.

Archiving the license partners' VOUCHER COPIES requires a carefully managed library structured according to the type of license. The translation archive is arranged by author, under author by language, under language by individual works in alphabetical order, and under individual works by publication date. This is the only way in which the 52 editions of Hesse's *Siddhartha* and its numerous reprints and sub-licenses across 52 languages can be catalogued. Should there be sufficient space and voucher copies, it makes sense to devote an additional library department to the most important license partners. The domestic license archive (book club, paperback and special editions) should also be sorted by author in chronological order. Here too, a supplementary library with an overview of the most important paperback partners is recommended, in particular if the publishing house generates a major share of its sales in this segment. Additionally, the non-print archive should be sorted according to narrators, actors and license partners.

The DESPATCH OF VOUCHER COPIES to the copyright owners as well as to the archives named by them must occur swiftly after publication. Archiving licensed editions is an indispensable component in the granting of future licenses and, over the years, achieves inestimable documentary value for the author's reception domestically and abroad. It forms the basis for new translations if the work in question has been out of print for a long period or only available from second-hand bookshops.

4.1
E-BOOKS

Technological progress, changes in the requirements and habits of media use and knowledge transfer, and the increased frequency of demand caused by globally operating equipment manufacturers, all represent a challenge for publishing houses to swiftly increase their product range of electronic publications, in particular, e-books.

The following series of questions can have an influence on the adjustment and evaluation of author's contracts both at home and abroad, especially concerning remuneration:

1. Should e-books be published within the own programme, i.e. under the label of the book publisher? Should the book publisher—as an imprint or as a joint venture with other publishers—set up a specialist e-book publishing house? Or do limited personnel, infrastructural, technical and production capacities in one's own publishing house make it necessary to grant e-book rights to third-party publishing houses as licenses?

2. What costs will arise regarding the production, distribution, sales, application, technical and administrative aspects of e-book front and backlist maintenance? Does the book publisher have the corresponding data and manuscripts or, as is often the case with backlist titles, do these have to be produced for the first time? Will conversion of the physical book manuscript to the e-book format (e-pub, etc.) and its derivatives (i.e. data formats of respective reading devices) take place in one's own production department or does a third-party service provider need to be assigned this task? Where applicable, will a new staff position for all work arising

from the production and distribution of e-books be created? What are the implications of maintaining bibliographic databases? What means does the publishing house's accounting department need in order to display electronic routes of distribution on royalty statements?

3. In cooperation with which partners does the distribution of e-books take place? Does the publishing house have its own reading device? Is it limited to cooperation with one manufacturer or Internet platform or is its aim to prepare its works for as many end-user devices as possible? Are stationery or Internet booksellers included in the supply chain? Which institutions involved in the end consumer price does the e-book pass through on the way from book publisher to reader?

4. How is the end consumer price of the e-book determined? Who specifies it—the book publisher, the equipment manufacturer, the download platform or the publisher in cooperation with its partners? Which price gap—from e-book to bound

edition and to paperback—is reasonable, enforceable and appropriate to the content? Are e-books liable to statutory fixed prices? Are the prices for the respective trade partners fixed where applicable for a certain period, or are they variable in the first place? Are end consumers offered subscription models or bundles?

5. How is the e-book (or data) equipped? What quality requirements does it have to meet for the book publisher or the end consumer? Does it contain simply the text itself, or does it offer search and commentary functions or, where applicable, additional material by other copyright owners? Are multimedia interfaces for film and audio documents offered? How can protection against illicit reproduction be guaranteed and to what extent is it practical?

6. Can the publisher offer e-books as a supplementary edition to the print editions, maintain the latter in at least one edition format, or does it intend where applicable to publish a work from the outset or in the future exclusively in electronic form? Should

and can (from the contractual perspective) works that are physically out of print be offered as e-books? Is a work deemed available with regard to the copyright holder or the foreign rights holder if only the non-physical edition can be obtained? Do sales of e-books have to reach a certain annual minimum to be regarded as available?

It is recommended that publishers take a calm approach. It is necessary to gather experience with individual e-book products: not every printed title is suited for digitization.

4.2
OPEN ACCESS

The open access movement is based on the wish of academics, universities and research communities to guarantee all users unrestricted, free access to academic publications. The advantages for academics and users alike are obvious and these can be found on the information portal open-access.net, among other sites. Book publishing houses are excluded from this procedure: there is no transfer of rights involved. The copyright owner retains all rights but he foregoes a fee.

Those affected are, first and foremost, academic and specialist publishing houses, primarily those that publish scientific works. As a rule, the author has already put his research results on the web before he transfers rights to a publishing house for publication. The transfer of the electronic rights to the publishing house as such is obsolete. Further dissemination of the work in digital databases occurs on the basis of open access, thereby eliminating the chance for the publishing house and the author to make economic use of the work.

4.3
NEW AND ESTABLISHED DUTIES

For publishing houses, the digital era ushers in new duties. The goals, however, remain the same:

- Long-term programme planning and author support
- Increased sales
- Specific support of distributors, booksellers and direct clients.

The duties outlined have been determined by the endeavours of international publishing houses through the centuries. The general goal has not changed as a result of new technical opportunities and types of use. Having considered the present situation and recollected traditional contract values, an additional volume will have to be devised in the coming years to charter further developments. Not least, it will be the reader and the reading habits of future generations who will decide which route the author and publishing house take together. Expectations of consumers worldwide regarding literature and science are diverse and open to discussion. The printed and electronic book will coexist in decades to come: they will be complementary entities, and, perhaps in certain market sectors, the e-book will supplant the printed book. The job of the publishing house will shift in this case almost entirely to production. In the value chain of copyright protection and the distribution of works, the appropriate remuneration of authors has to uphold the standard that, via the printed book, made the book industry what it still is today: a pioneer of new content in the arena of culture.

5
APPENDICES

APPENDIX A: A SAMPLE ROYALTY SCALE

1. In-house writers

(a) Hardback (original) edition

10% up to 50,000 copies

12% thereafter

(b) Paperback edition

First use/original editions

7% for all copies

First use/special formats

6% up to 25,000 copies

7% up to 50,000 copies

8% up to 100,000 copies

10% thereafter

Second use	5% up to 10,000 copies
	6% up to 20,000 copies
	7% thereafter
(c) Series, hardback	7.5% for all copies
(d) Special editions	8% for all editions in the hardback segment
	5% for all paperback editions

---

2. International agencies and foreign publishers

(a) Hardback editions	6% up to 5,000 copies
	7% up to 10,000 copies
	8% up to 50,000 copies
	10% thereafter
(b) Paperbacks	5% up to 25,000 copies
	6% up to 50,000 copies
	7% thereafter
(c) Paperback special formats	6% up to 25,000 copies
	7% up to 50,000 copies
	8% up to 100,000 copies
	10% thereafter

1. AUTHOR CONTRACT

NAME and ADDRESS
(hereafter known as 'the Publisher')
on the one part

and
NAME and ADDRESS
(hereafter known as 'the Author')
on the other part

agree to the following
Author Agreement

The rights and obligations set forth herein shall also apply to the legal heirs and successors to each of the parties to the Agreement. To testify their consent, the parties have signed two identical copies hereof; and each party to the Agreement has received one copy.

1.	**The Manuscript**
1.1	The object of this Agreement is the present/ existing or yet-to-be-written Work by the Author, entitled ____ (TITLE) (hereafter known as 'the Work')

1.2   The Author grants and assigns the Publisher the sole and exclusive right for all language publications to print, publish and otherwise reproduce, distribute and sell the Work throughout the world for the first and all subsequent print runs and editions, and during the legal term of copyright.

1.3   The Publisher agrees to print and publish the Work, to apply due care in its production, to advertise the book, and to assure optimal distribution among both booksellers and the public. The Publisher agrees to exercise the utilization rights for the Work as granted in this Agreement in the best interests of the Author. The Author warrants that his Work does not violate or infringe any rights of third parties, that she or he is the sole holder of the rights and that she or he has not hitherto granted rights to other parties that could oppose those stipulated in this Agreement. In doing so, she or he exempts the Publisher from any claims from third parties including the costs of potential legal proceedings and/or litigation.

1.4   The Author agrees to indicate to the Publisher any depiction of persons or events in the Work that carry a potential risk of personality rights infringement or any other rights infringement. The Author is obliged to make any changes requested by the Publisher on this matter. Only if the Author has fulfilled this obligation to the full extent of her or his knowledge and conscience shall the Publisher carry the costs of a potential legal proceeding and/or litigation.

1.5   The Author agrees to deliver the completed manuscript in electronic data form to the Publisher by _____ (DATE) at the latest, fulfilling all necessary requirements of a manuscript prepared for typesetting (style-sheet and formatting requirements in the most current format). The anticipated length of the Work is approximately _____ PAGES.

1.6   The Author shall keep an electronic copy and a physical copy of the manuscript for her or himself. Due to the existence of this backup copy, claims for compensation due to loss of the manuscript are excluded.

1.7   Should the manuscript feature quality defects or should the manuscript deviate from the requirements stipulated in Clause 1.5, the Author is obliged to make revisions within a reasonable period of time determined by the Publisher. In the case that changes authorized and desired by the Publisher are not or cannot be made despite requests, the Publisher is authorized to make the changes either through the editorial office or an appropriate third party while safeguarding the Author's moral rights whereby the Publisher reserves the right to retain a part of the costs incurred from the Author's fee or to rescind the Agreement. Corrections suggested by the editorial office and accepted by the Author shall be transferred by the Author to the electronic version of his or her manuscript upon Publisher's request.

2   **Grant of Rights**

2.1   The Author grants the Publisher the sole and
           exclusive rights throughout the world for print-
           ing, publishing, reproducing, distributing and
           selling of the Work during the legal term of
           copyright in all known forms of utilization,
           both for the Publisher itself and its licensees for
           all issues and editions without restriction in
           quantity and in particular:

2.1.1   the right to print, publish and sell the Work in
           hardcover, paperback, paper-bound, large-
           print, schoolbook, special, reader, luxury,
           reprint and book club and other editions;

2.1.2   the right to translate the Work into other
           languages and to render it in other dialects and
           the right to utilize these language versions in
           any form covered by the Agreement;

2.1.3   the right to produce the Work in whole or part
           thereof as a pre-print (first serial rights) or
           reprint (second serial rights), as well as serial
           printing in periodicals (e.g. newspapers, jour-
           nals) and in non-periodical publications includ-
           ing necessary adjustments for electronic media
           or advertising purposes, even when no print fee
           is realized, and to include the Work in whole or
           part thereof in anthologies and calendars;

2.1.4   the right to publish and distribute the Work in
           any other way, most notably by means of digi-
           tal, photomechanical or similar procedures
           (e.g. Braille, (digital) photocopy);

2.1.5   the right to publish and distribute or make
           accessible the Work as a whole or part thereof

as a non-physical e-book as well as storing it in machine-readable form in an appropriate data format on the Publisher's data bank or on the electronic data bank of an authorized third party and/or data networks including links to other works and making the Work accessible to numerous users as a whole or part thereof by means of digital or different storage and transmission technology including page or chapter excerpts on individual demand for reproduction, download and/or print-out irrespective of transmission system (e. g. Internet, mobile telephone) and type of receiver (e.g. computer, tablet PC, mobile telephone, e-book reader, smartphone or any other form of mobile or stationary—including multifunctional—terminal), and namely for an unrestricted number of transmissions, retrievals and renditions. This includes the right to allow the user the interactive utilization of the Work or parts thereof (and if necessary in combination with various editions of the Work) and to supplement the Work with—where necessary multimedia—work-specific materials;

2.1.6   the right to publish and distribute electronic editions of the Work as a whole or parts thereof on an unrestricted number of physical data-storage media irrespective of technical equipment and including all digital or interactive systems (e.g. CD-ROM, CD, CD-I, DVD, memory card among others);

2.1.7   the right to recite (e.g. public reading) the Work (as a whole or part thereof) by third parties including the right to record the recital on any kind of data-storage system and to sell the edition of the Work in any form covered by the Agreement;

2.1.8   the right to adapt the Work as an audio book and/or radio play (e.g. in the form of a shortened recital, in dramatized form with several voices, with or without music, etc.) and the utilization of the audio-book edition in any form covered by the Agreement, especially the publishing and distributing on sound-storage media, image-storage media and other physical-storage media (e.g. all CD formats, MP3 data media, memory cards) as well as the provision of a non-physical audio-book edition for numerous users for individual retrieval (e.g. streaming, download to any kind of stationary or mobile receiver including multi-functional receivers);

2.1.9   the right to adapt the Work as a comic and/or graphic novel as well as the right to publish and distribute these works and to utilize them in any form covered by the Agreement;

2.1.10   the right to use the Work for a one-off or repeated production for a theatre play, choreography or any other form of performing art as well as the right to perform these versions of the Work on stage and to utilize them in any form covered by the Agreement. The Publisher shall exercise such rights only after obtaining Author's approval;

2.1.11   the right to film and TV productions including script rights and performances in cinemas as well as TV broadcasts of productions created in this way, videogram rights (in particular video, DVD) and the right to the provision of retrieval and exploitation of the filming in any form covered by the Agreement. This includes remake rights, title use rights, synchronization rights, clipping rights and the right to reproduce the production in book form. The Publisher shall exercise the film rights only after obtaining the Author's approval;

2.1.12 broadcasting rights, i.e. the right to broadcast the Work in any form covered by the Agreement on terrestrial radio, (TV, radio), cable, satellite, mobile phone and similar broadcasting techniques or via Internet (live-streaming); in addition, the rights of reproduction or soundtrack resulting from the Work or its image- or audio-tape anchorage or due to loudspeaker transmission or broadcast accruing reproduction, playback and transferring rights;

2.1.13 the right to set the Work to music or opera and the right to exploit this music/opera in any form covered by the Agreement;

2.1.14 the right to commercial or non-commercial lending or rental of all physical book editions as well as all audio, image/audio and other physical data-storage media rights as covered in this Agreement;

2.1.15 the right to print or broadcast or otherwise reproduce the Work as a whole or part thereof within the scope of the rights granted including the Internet (audio sample, reading excerpt, book trailer, etc.), to advertise the Work including non-remunerated uses; the right to reproduce the Work on the Publisher's own or foreign databank platforms, to index the Work and make it accessible in part to users for content research and reading samples;

2.1.16   merchandising rights, i.e. the right to commercial exploitation of the Work and its parts via production and distribution of products of all kinds using characters, names, events, plot, titles, texts, illustrations and drawings contained in the Work and the right to advertise for goods and services of all kinds by using such elements as well as applications for trademarks as seen fit; this includes the right to exploit the Work or its parts via production and distribution of computer games and any other multimedia productions; the Publisher shall exercise such rights only after obtaining the Author's approval.

2.2   Furthermore, the Author also grants the Publisher the sole and exclusive rights throughout the world for any unknown types of rights at the time of the conclusion of the Agreement. In the case that the Publisher utilizes these rights (itself or its licensees), the Author shall receive appropriate remuneration, which is to be mutually agreed by both parties in the event of an intended inclusion of rights by the Publisher. In cases of doubt, the Publisher is permitted to determine the remuneration at equitable discretion.

2.3   In the evaluation and administration of the rights named in Clauses 2.1 and 2.2, the Publisher is authorized but not obliged to utilize rights according to remuneration guidelines set down by law where these are utilized by the Publisher itself or where exclusive or single-use rights are granted to licensees where nothing to the contrary is stipulated in this Agreement. This includes the commissioning of collecting societies or agencies.

2.4   The Author hereby agrees that the Publisher may grant rights of production of paperback, special and schoolbook editions to its affiliated publishing houses. For such editions, the usual royalties of the affiliated publishing houses apply. The relevant statements shall be made in accordance with Clause 3.7 directly to the publisher utilizing the right.

2.5   The right of the Publisher to grant rights of use to third parties expires with the termination of this Agreement. The stock of licence agreements that have already been concluded is not affected by this clause. The statements of licensing revenue shall take place according to the existing royalty guidelines (Clauses 3.4–3.8).

3   **Advances and Royalties**

3.1   The Author shall receive from Publisher a one-off advance payment of _____, which is to be offset against all earnings and royalties stipulated in this Agreement. The advance payment shall be paid in the following payment term: _____.

3.2   The Author shall receive the following royalties for a Publisher's own utilization of the rights granted:

3.2.1   as trade edition:

____ % for the first ____ copies

____ % for all copies sold thereafter;

3.2.2   as book edition in the series:

SERIES 1:

SERIES 2:

SERIES 3:

3.2.3   for all special and paper-bound editions in the

• core series:

• paperback series:

3.2.4   as graphic novel:

from the retail price less VAT of every sold, paid and not returned copy;

3.2.5   as non-physical electronic edition (especially e-book) according to Clause 2.1.5 **20%** of the Publisher's net receipts.

3.3   For all other forms of utilization by the Publisher and editions of the Work, the Author shall receive appropriate remuneration, which is to be mutually agreed by both parties. In the event of an intended inclusion of rights by the Publisher, the Author shall be notified.

3.4   The Author shall receive remuneration in form of a share of the Publisher's net proceeds for utilization of rights that are not exercised by the Publisher (after deduction of costs carried by the Publisher such as agency fees, foreign taxes, third party fees, etc.). The Author shall receive:

3.4.1   for the utilization of rights from Clauses 2.1.1, 2.1.3 and 2.1.5, in as far as these involve licences for German-language editions at home and abroad: **50%**;

3.4.2   for the utilization of all other rights: **70%**;

3.4.3   In case the Publisher has to pay a third party for the adaptation of the Work to the stage in the utilization of rights according to Clause 2.1.10, the Author shall receive remuneration differing from the above: **50%**.

Statements and Payments

3.5   Proceeds from granting rights abroad shall be processed in ___ (LOCAL CURRENCY) if nothing to the contrary is agreed.

3.6   In accordance with the SALES TAX ACT, the royalties shall be increased to include the VAT applicable at any one time, where the Author pays tax on these sales in accordance with this law (standard taxation procedure). The Author hereby declares that she or he is/is not currently subject to standard taxation procedures (whichever does not apply should to be deleted; otherwise 'is not subject to' shall apply). The Author shall notify the Publisher without delay of any changes to the taxation of his or her royalty income.

3.7   Statements of account and payments shall take place twice a year, namely on 30 June and 31 December within the following 60 days. The first invoice will take place on the deadline that falls at least 6 months after the date of publication of the Work. A payment shall only take place if the invoice reaches a sum of at least € 50. Lower sums will be added to the next statement. Statements from licensees will only be respected if the respective payment (that the Publisher is obliged to insure) has already taken place. Otherwise statements and payment on the part of the Publisher will take place in the next six-monthly statement.

Author account number:
Name and address of bank:
Sort code:

3.8   The Publisher is permitted to deduct remuneration from following invoices for copies that have been invoiced to the Author as sold but later returned. Insofar as the advanced payment according to Clause 3.1 can be fully cleared, the Publisher is permitted to deduct claims for remuneration from other agreements between the Author and Publisher. The Publisher is permitted after the first serial of Publisher's own book editions to retain up to 10% of the invoice sum in case of potential returns. The retained sum shall be invoiced 18 months after the first invoice and paid as long as it does not have to be cleared against returns.

3.9   The Author may demand that the Publisher certify his accounting by a chartered accountant; the costs of this certification shall be carried by the Publisher if the accounting proves to be erroneous by more than 5% to the detriment of the Author; in other cases, the costs shall be carried by the Author.

3.10 After the death of the Author, claims for remuneration shall continue via production of a certificate of inheritance by an authorized heir, who shall be named as power of attorney by a majority of heirs, and who must be responsible for all other matter regarding questions in relation to the contractual partner. Until a power of attorney is named by a group of heirs and instructions for payment have been received, the Publisher is permitted to retain remuneration without interest resulting from royalties owed.

4   **Rights and Obligations of the Publisher**

4.1 The Publisher is obliged to print and publish its own editions as stipulated in Clauses 3.2.1, 3.2.2 and 3.2.5. Nevertheless, the Publisher is permitted but not obliged to utilize the rights laid down in this Agreement.

4.2 The first publication is planned within: ___ (NAME OF SERIES)

4.3 The Publisher determines the date of publication, the features (particularly layout, typography and cover design) and/or the format, the retail price as well as the number of the print run for electronic publications for the first and all other editions. The right of the Publisher to determine the retail price at discretion rules out later increases or decreases in price.

4.4 The final title shall be decided upon in agreement with the Publisher and Author. If an agreement is not reached, the Publisher shall decide in accordance with the moral rights of the Author.

4.5   The Publisher is obliged to indicate the Author as the copyright owner of the Work.

5   Typesetting and Corrections

5.1   The Publisher shall and may correct common composition errors. The Author shall correct the proof-sheets, which shall be sent to him or her and provide the revised proofs with the note 'ready for press'. This note includes the approval for any variations from the manuscript and it has to be granted at least two weeks after mailing. If the Author does not make a declaration within three weeks after mailing, the proof shall be considered 'ready for press'.

5.2   If the Author makes alterations in the completed typesetting, which are more extensive than the elimination of composition errors, she or he has to defray additional charges at the Publisher's net cost price, insofar as they exceed 20% of the typesetting charges for the complete Work.

6   Author's and Promotional Copies

6.1   The Publisher reserves the right to produce additional, royalty-free copies at its discretion, totalling up to 20% of each print run in the form of statutory deposits, promotional, review and house copies. The Publisher shall not be required to provide proof as to how such copies are used.

6.2   The Author shall receive ___ COPIES from the first print run as complimentary copies; and ___ COPIES as complimentary copies from each subsequent print run. The Author is authorized to purchase further copies from the Publisher at a discount of 40%. When purchasing from the Publisher and affiliated publishing companies, the Author shall receive a discount of 35% (except on bibliophilic editions).

6.3   The Publisher will make the Author aware of reviews received if requested.

7   **Remainder Copies**

7.1   In the event that at least 3 years after its original publication, sales of the Work decline to such an extent that the Publisher deems further distribution of the Work no longer worthwhile, the Publisher has the right to sell off or pulp the remaining stocks of the Work in whole or in part. Author shall be remunerated with 10% of the net receipts from the remaining sell-off.

7.2   The Publisher agrees to give the Author advance notification of any such intention to enable him or her to acquire the remaining stocks, in whole or in part, at manufacturing cost. The Publisher is relieved of this obligation if only a part of the remaining stocks of the Work is about to be sold off or pulped.

8   **Termination and Reversion of Rights**

8.1   In the event that the Publisher fails to keep the Work available in any of the editions according to Clauses 3.2.1, 3.2.2, 3.2.3 and 3.2.5 and if ___ (LANGUAGE) editions by third parties are not available any more either, the Author may request the Publisher by written notice to declare, within 3 months of receiving the request, to resume utilization of the work in any of the editions mentioned within a period of 1 year after the expiration of the 3-month time limit. If the Publisher does not fulfil the agreed obligations on time or if the time limit for a re-utilization is exceeded, the Author may rescind this Agreement in writing. The assertion of this termination right on the part of the Author is conditional upon the Author refunding any advances against royalties that have not yet been offset by sales of the Work.

8.2   If this Agreement ends prematurely due to withdrawal or constructive dismissal, the Publisher is allowed to distribute already printed but undelivered copies of its own editions of the Work up to 1 year after the point of time when the withdrawal or constructive dismissal comes into force.

9   General Terms

9.1   This Agreement shall be governed and construed in accordance with the laws of ___ (NAME OF COUNTRY), most notably the copyright and publishing laws of ___ (NAME OF COUNTRY).

9.2   All changes and additions to this Agreement are only valid in writing. This also applies if this requirement shall be revoked.

9.3   Should one or more individual parts of this contract be or become null and void, invalid or contestable entirely or partly, the validity of the remaining contract shall remain unaffected. In lieu of an invalid provision, a valid provision which corresponds to the intent and purpose of the invalid provision shall be agreed upon. In case of incompleteness, a provision shall be agreed upon in which in conformity with intent and purpose of these provisions would have been agreed upon if the parties had originally considered such matter.

9.4   The Publisher and the Author agree to inform each other if they perceive any potential violation of rights granted within this Agreement and to take appropriate measures themselves.

9.5   Place of performance and jurisdiction for all matters issuing from this Agreement shall be exclusively ___ (NAME OF CITY).

9.6   Should the Author live outside the territory of ___ (NAME OF COUNTRY) or move there or should his or her residence be unknown or if the Author is a businessman or a corporate body under public law, the sole and exclusive place of performance and jurisdiction for charges, asserted by entering an action, is the registered office of the Publisher: ___ (NAME OF CITY).

Author   Publisher

PLACE, DATE   PLACE, DATE

Addendum to the contract dated ____
(hereafter known as the 'Contract')

between
NAME and ADDRESS
(hereafter known as 'the Publisher')
on the one part

and
NAME and ADDRESS,
(hereafter known as 'the Author')
on the other part

concerning the work entitled
TITLE
(hereafter known as 'the Work').

1   **Grant of Rights**
In acceptance to the terms and conditions covering the assignment of rights and other arrangements stipulated in the Contract dated ____, the Author additionally grants the Publisher the exclusive electronic rights for the Work for the comprehensive utilization of the Work without restrictions of time, territory or

in number of physical and non-physical electronic form, specifically

1.1   the right to reproduce the Work for all types of use stipulated in the Contract as an electronic edition (e.g. e-book, audio book or file) and to distribute it and/or make it available, hence record it in an appropriate, machine-readable data format on the Publisher's or third-party electronic databases and/or data networks, also in connection with other works; to store it and make it accessible to an unlimited number of users either in part or as a whole; to make it available by page or by chapter according to individual requests for reproduction as a download and/or print-out regardless of the transmission system (e.g. Internet or mobile telephone) and the type of receiving appliance (e.g. computer, cellphone, e-book reader, iPod or other forms of mobile or stationary—as well as multi-functional terminal device); and/or to publish it on physical data carriers (CD-ROM, CD, DVD, memory card, etc.);

1.2   The Publisher has the right to facilitate an interactive use of the Work, or parts of it—if necessary in connection with varying electronic versions of the Work, and to complement the Work through (where relevant, multimedia) materials specific to the Work.

1.3   the right to index the Work in electronic form for the purposes of sales promotion and to provide it with search functions that allow a text search to be carried out in the Work and allow users to gain an impression free of charge via electronic book search programmes and/or carry out content searches in the Work. The Publisher shall ensure that the content available is limited;

1.4 the right to promote the Work within the range of the rights conferred in all types of use stipulated in the Contract including the Internet (e.g. extracts, video trailers, audio samples);

1.5 the right to edit the Work insofar as this is technically necessary to fulfil the purposes of the above-mentioned rights.

1.6 The author shall furthermore grant the Publisher exclusive rights of use, without restrictions on territory and content, for types of use unidentified at the time of the conclusion of this addendum for the period of the Contract.

1.7 Place of performance and jurisdiction for all matters issuing from this Agreement shall be exclusively ____ (NAME OF CITY).

2 **Royalties**

2.1 For the Publisher's own physical and non-physical electronic editions (e.g. e-books) according to Clause 1.1, the Author shall receive a fee of 20% of the Publisher's net proceeds (less VAT).

2.2 When allocating the above-mentioned rights according to Clause 1.1 in the form of a licence to third parties for physical and non-physical electronic editions, the author shall receive a share of 50% of the Publisher's net proceeds.

2.3   As remuneration for the granting of rights of use according to Clause 1.6) (unidentified types of use), the author shall receive appropriate remuneration, to which the parties shall agree once there is an intended inclusion of rights by the Publisher or its licensee.

2.4   Settlement and payment will proceed according to the provisions made in the Publisher's Contract.

Author   Publisher
PLACE, DATE   PLACE, DATE

MEMORANDUM OF AGREEMENT
made this _____ (DATE) between

NAME AND ADDRESS
(hereafter known as 'the Proprietor')
of the one part,

and
NAME AND ADDRESS
(hereafter known as 'the Publisher')
on the other part

whereby it is mutually agreed as follows respecting
a work entitled

TITLE
(hereafter known as 'the Work')

In consideration of the mutual promises hereafter set
forth, the parties do agree as follows:

1   **Grant of Rights**

      The Proprietor hereby grants to the Publisher
for a period of ___ (DURATION) years of the
date of execution of this Agreement the sole and
exclusive right to print, publish and distribute
in print form (hardcover, paperback, . . .), electronic form (see Clause 17) and audio-book

form the _____ (LANGUAGE) translation of the Work in the following territory: throughout the world.

2   **Warranties**

2.1   The Proprietor represents and warrants that the Proprietor has the right to grant the rights set forth in this Agreement and that to the best of its knowledge the Work does not contain any material that would be libelous or defamatory under ___ NAME OF COUNTRY's law.

2.2   The Publisher hereby absolves the Proprietor and the author of any responsibility from any liability arising from the Publisher's publication of the Work. The Publisher, at its own expense, will be responsible for obtaining permission, where necessary, for use in the Publisher's edition of the Work of photographs, illustrations, quotations or other copyrighted material obtained by the Proprietor from other sources.

3   **Publication Term**

The Publisher agrees to translate and publish the Work at their own expense within 24 months from the date of execution of this Agreement. If the Publisher fails to publish the said translation within said period, all rights granted to the Publisher shall automatically revert to the Proprietor for its use, benefit and disposition and this contract shall be considered null and void, except that the Proprietor may retain the advance paid to it by the Publisher whose financial obligations which are already executed remain in force.

4	**Translation**
4.1	The translation of the Work shall be made faithfully and accurately by a translator of the highest standard from the _____ original. No abbreviations, additions or alterations in the text, photographs or title may be made without prior written approval of the Proprietor.
4.2	The licence edition must follow in every respect exactly the original edition as published by the Proprietor regarding sections, paragraphs, running heads, position of notes, etc. This means that also any preface or introduction or afterword or commentaries or notes by the translator or the Publisher's editor—provided the Proprietor has approved of it and given permission in writing—must be placed apart from the corpus of the Work and clearly be recognizable as not being part of the original edition of the Work.
4.3	The Publisher shall submit its translation of the Work to the Proprietor for written approval and shall work closely with the Proprietor in every respect with regard to the translation and accept her or his jurisdiction on this matter. The Proprietor shall be allowed 4 weeks from receipt of translation to respond.
4.4	The choice of the translator is subject to prior written approval of the Proprietor. The translation of the Work will be made by ___ (NAME OF TRANSLATOR). Any change in translator will be subject to prior written approval by the Proprietor.

5   **Advance**

In consideration of the rights granted by the Proprietor, the Publisher agree to pay or cause to be paid on signature/half on signature, half on publication/on publication of this Agreement a non-refundable advance of € ____ against and on account of the royalties mentioned in Clause 6 only/and all further earnings.

6   **Royalties**

6.1   The royalties for the physical print editions will be calculated on the retail price less VAT/publishing price of the Publisher's editions of the Work:

6.1.1 Trade edition:
- 7% on the first 5,000 copies sold
- 8% from 5,001 to 8,000 copies sold
- 9% from 8,001 to 12,000 copies sold
- 10% on all copies sold thereafter

6.1.2 Pocketbook edition:
- 5% on the first 25,000 copies sold
- 6% on all copies sold thereafter

6.1.3 Audio-book edition:
- 10% on the first 5000 copies sold
- 11% from 5001 to 8000 copies sold
- 12% on all copies sold thereafter

6.2   On remainder copies sold by the Publisher at or below cost of manufacturing a share of 10% of gross incomes be payable to the Proprietor, but no such remainder copies shall be sold prior to 2 years from the date of each of Publisher's edition of the Work.

6.3 No royalties shall be payable on copies of Publisher's edition of the Work which are

(a) furnished gratis to the Author or

(b) distributed gratis for review, sample or other similar purposes, the number of such copies not to exceed 5% of any print run, or

(c) on copies destroyed.

6.4 For each e-book unit sold by or on behalf of the Publisher, as specified in Clause 17, whether as a whole or limited to parts of the text, the Publisher shall pay the following royalty to the Proprietor:

• 25% of the Publisher's net receipts. By net receipts it should be understood all receipts, net only of the discount to distributors and/or retailers, if any, such discounts not to exceed 50% of the full published recommended download price and any legally required sales tax such as VAT.

• [or] 20% of the download price paid by the customer less any legally required sales tax such as VAT.

6.5 The Publisher shall inform the Proprietor of the price of the e-book of the Work and any further change. Unless otherwise mutually agreed, the Publisher shall publish the e-book at a price of no less than 75% of the recommended retail price of the Publisher's prevailing print edition of the Work.

7   **Subsidiary Rights**

        No Subsidiary rights are granted under this
        Agreement/[or]

7.1   Subject to the Proprietor's prior written
        approval, in each instance the Publisher is
        authorized to licence the following rights in
        the Publisher's edition of the Work in the
        territory and the gross proceeds from the
        disposal of such rights shall be shared between
        the Proprietor and the Publisher as follows:

        • Pre-publication rights
          Proprietor: 60%   Publisher: 40%

        • Post-publication serial rights
          Proprietor: 60%   Publisher: 40%

        • Book Club rights
          Proprietor: 60%   Publisher: 40%

        • Cheap Edition rights
          Proprietor: 60%   Publisher: 40%

        • Kiosk rights
          Proprietor: 60%   Publisher: 40%

        • Mass-market paperback
          Proprietor: 60%   Publisher: 40%

        • Audio book
          (single voice, straight reading unabridged)
          Proprietor: 60%   Publisher: 40%

        • TV + Radio
          (single voice straight reading unabridged)
          Proprietor: 60%   Publisher: 40%

        • Anthology and Quotations
          Proprietor: 60%   Publisher: 40%

        In the event that the company to which any of

these subsidiary rights is granted is owned by the Publisher, then the Proprietor shall receive 100% of the Publisher's gross proceeds from such subsidiary licences.

7.2   Further to the above-mentioned subsidiary rights, the Proprietor grants to Publisher the right to use up to 20% but not more than 20 pages from the Work in ___ translation purely for promotional and marketing purposes on-line, on its own homepage and that of major booksellers and book promoters.

7.3   The Publisher shall accept offers for subsidiary rights only for limited duration not exceeding the duration of this Agreement by more than 1 year. On termination of this Agreement, Publisher will inform its licensees that renewals of any sub-licence agreements should be negotiated with the Proprietor, and that payments and statements are to be sent to the Proprietor directly. It is understood that sub-licences may not licence any rights to further parties.

7.4   The Publisher shall provide the Proprietor with a copy of each sub-licence contract promptly after it execution with the exception of anthology and quotation permissions.

7.5   No income due to the subsidiary rights granted by the Proprietor in this clause shall be held against the advance payment as specified under Clause 5.

8   **Reservation of Rights**

All rights either now existing or which may come into existence, which are not specifically granted to the Publisher in this Agreement, are hereby reserved to and by the Proprietor for its use and disposition at any time.

9	**Accounting**
9.1	The Publisher agrees to keep accurate books showing the number of sales and amounts realized from any publication under this Agreement or any subsidiary rights income according to Clause 7 and to render accountings and payment to the Proprietor by wire transfer only annually on 1 March for the period ending 31 December/semi-annually on 1 March and 1 September for the periods ending 30 June and 31 December and to submit certified copies of such accountings to the Proprietor and to permit the Proprietor or anyone designated by it to inspect such books of accounting.
9.2	No income due to the Proprietor under this Agreement shall be cross collateralized or held against any amount due to the Proprietor from any other Agreement that may exist between the Proprietor and the Publisher.
10	**Copyright**

The original title of the Work and the following copyright shall be printed on the verso of the title page of every copy of the Publisher's edition of the Work:

© Rights owner, Place/Year.

All rights reserved by and controlled through ___ (NAME OF PUBLISHER AND PLACE).

The Publisher shall not do any act or permit any act to be done which will cause its edition to fall into the public domain in any country in which such edition shall be published or distributed.

11	**Credits and Advertising**

11.1   The name of the author shall appear in its customary form in due prominence on the title page, the cover jacket and on the binding of every copy of the Publisher's edition; in all advertising and promotional material and on all editions licensed by the Publisher. The name(s) of the editor(s) of the original edition shall appear in its customary form in due prominence on the title page and in all editions licensed by the Publisher.

11.2   The Proprietor shall comment on the jacket/ cover design of the Publisher's editions of the Work and shall be given 10 working days from receipt of material to respond. The Proprietor's suggestions shall be considered by the Publisher wherever possible.

11.3   The Publisher shall not print advertisements of any kind or for any other book other than by the Author in any edition of the Work or on the jacket/cover without the Proprietor's prior written approval.

12	**Complimentary Copies**

The Publisher agrees to deliver 6 copies of the first print run, 1 copy of each subsequent print run of the Work published by the Publisher and 1 copy of each licensed edition to the Proprietor at the above-mentioned address. The Proprietor shall have the right to purchase further copies at the usual trade discount.

13 **Termination**

13.1 This contract shall come into effect upon execution of this Agreement by both parties and the payment of the sum due under Clause 3 of this Agreement to the Proprietor.

13.2 All rights granted under this Agreement revert to the Proprietor if during the validity of the Agreement:

(a) the Publisher has less than 100 copies of any of its physical print editions of the Work in stock.

(b) after 5 years from the first publication of the Work less than 50 copies of any of its physical print editions are sold in any calendar year. For electronic editions, see Clause 17.

13.3 Rights for the respective edition revert if it is unobtainable and the Publisher does not within 30 days after receipt of written notice from the Proprietor indicate that it will reprint and publish the respective edition within 6 months. For electronic editions, see Clause 17.

13.4 Upon the occurrence of any of the events set forth in parts (13.2a) or (13.2b) the rights granted to the Publisher shall automatically revert to the Proprietor, without further notice, to be used and disposed of as the Proprietor shall determine.

13.5 Should the Publisher be declared bankrupt or insolvent or enter into a composition with its creditors or suffer the appointment of a receiver, or should it violate or fail to fulfil any of the terms of this Agreement and not rectify such violation or act within 1 month of having received written notice from the Proprietor to do so, then all rights granted under this Agreement shall revert to the Proprietor who shall be entitled to dispose of the rights set forth in this Agreement as the Proprietor may determine. However, the Publisher shall remain obligated to continue to pay the Proprietor its share of whatever income it receives from previous licences granted to a third party.

13.6 A violation of any clause in this Agreement shall automatically end the contract, which shall be considered null and void, except that the Proprietor may retain the advance paid to it by the Publisher whose financial obligations which are already executed remain in force.

13.7 All rights granted to the Publisher under this Agreement will automatically and without further notice revert to the Proprietor on ___ (DATE) unless a new Agreement is agreed to in writing by both parties.

14 **Non-Transferable Rights**

Neither this Agreement nor the rights and licences granted to the Publisher can be transferred or assigned by the Publisher. All of the Publisher's obligations and rights are personal and non-assignable.

15   **Applicable Law**

This Agreement is binding and inures to the benefit of the successors and assigns of the Proprietor. This Agreement shall be interpreted according to the laws of the ___ (NAME OF COUNTRY). The place of performance and jurisdiction shall be ___ (NAME OF CITY).

16   **Execution of the Agreement**

16.1   This contractual offer becomes automatically null and void if the Proprietor is not in receipt of the duly signed contract copies within a period of 6 weeks.

16.2   Should the Proprietor not receive the advance payment within 4 weeks from the date of this Agreement, the Agreement shall be rendered invalid and all rights shall automatically revert to the Proprietor's free disposition.

17   **Electronic Rights**

17.1   The Publisher shall have the exclusive right to produce, publish and sell the Work in e-book form as specified below.

17.2   An e-book is the unabridged verbatim sequential reproduction of the text of the Work. The text of the e-book emulates print reproduction, may or may not include a search facility and is encrypted for downloads. The Publisher shall have the right to issue the e-book by way of any secure electronic, magnetic, digital or optical online or offline database platforms with customized accessibility owned by the Publisher and/or third parties on a service basis, capable of storing and/or transmitting the e-book, making it available to be displayed and read securely as a 'book' on a screen, whether on computers, smart phones, e-readers or any other suitable devices for single use, rental or educational and library use but not for resale. The Publisher shall determine the content visible to the user as a whole or limited to parts of the text only (e.g. chapter by chapter, page by page). It is understood that both the Proprietor and the Publisher share a common interest against abuse and undermining the sales of the Work under licence.

17.3   In addition to the subsidiary rights granted under Clause 7 of this Agreement, and subject to all restrictions set forth in this Agreement for the grant of subsidiary rights, the Publisher are authorized to licence electronic rights (such as Internet anthology rights, advertising on platforms and/or digital libraries, library distribution of digital verbatim content on platforms and/or digital libraries) and e-book rights to third parties. It is understood that a sub-licence of e-book rights means that the e-book is produced, published and distributed by a third party and that the e-book does in no way bear the Publisher's name. Any revenue generated from the sub-licence of these rights shall be shared 60:40 in favour of the Proprietor, unless the Proprietor receives an equal share separately and directly from the source of such revenue or through national registries.

17.4   The Publisher shall not market directly or promote e-book editions of the Work specifically to customers located in countries outside the territory granted to the Publisher under the terms of the Agreement.

17.5   In exercising the e-book rights, the Publisher shall make no changes of any kind to the Work without the prior written consent of the Proprietor. Every copy or part of the e-book shall bear the copyright notice of the Work as it appears in the print edition.

17.6   The granted rights do not include 'interactive multimedia rights'. No additional material in any form and no advertisements shall be included in the e-book without the Proprietor's prior approval in writing.

17.7   The Publisher shall ensure that the e-book shall be technically protected against manipulation and uncontrolled file sharing through a disclaimer, DRM technology and/or any other method suited to ensuring protection of the e-book. The Proprietor and the Publisher may at any time request a security audit on the database platforms. In the event that such security audit indicates serious security flaws, access to the e-book shall be immediately severed until an appropriate protection is demonstrably installed. While it is understood by both parties that there is no total security, illegal copying should be made very cumbersome and require exceptional technical skills. The Publisher shall be under obligation to pursue any form of abuse and pirating of the Work emanating from the rights granted in this Addendum within their reasonable legal means and economic possibilities.

17.8   The e-book rights herewith granted shall in no way be construed to include, to limit or to compete with any audio, audiovisual, interactive, multimedia, dramatic, merchandising, commercial, TV or motion picture or allied commercial rights.

17.9   The Publisher shall inform the Proprietor as soon as an e-book edition of the Work has been issued and will provide the Proprietor with one data file each of any e-book edition of the Work.

17.20 The Proprietor shall bear no direct or indirect expenses in connection with the production and marketing of the e-books.

17.21 Accounts of e-book sales shall be made according to Clause 9 and will specify the distribution partners, the number of units sold and related prices as well as any discounts to any distributors and/or retailers.

17.22 If the Publisher's account for less than a total of 50 sales units of any e-book edition of the Work in each calendar year, all electronic rights granted to the Publisher under this Agreement shall automatically revert to the Proprietor, without further notice, to be used and disposed of as Proprietor shall determine.

17.23 Upon termination of the grant of e-book rights the Publisher shall ensure that the digital publication of all e-books and all other electronic exploitations shall be shut down.

APPENDIX C: SOME USEFUL WEBSITES

London Book Fair
www.londonbookfair.co.uk

Turin Book Fair
www.fieralibro.it

Federation of European Publishers
www.fep-bee.be

Frankfurt Book Fair
www.buchmesse.de/de/fbm

Frankfurt Book Fair, Rights Directors Meeting:
www.buchmesse.de/de/networking/seminare_
konferenzen/rdm/

Goethe-Institut
www.goethe.de

International Association of Scientific, Technical &
Medical Publishers: www.stm-assoc.org

International Publishers Association:
www.internationalpublishers.org/index.php

Children's Book Fair, Bologna
www.bookfair.bolognafiere.it

Leipzig Book Fair
www.leipziger-buchmesse.de

Literarisches Colloquim Berlin
www.lcb.de

PEN International
www.internationalpen.org.uk/

Publishers Association
www.publishers.org.uk/

The Association of American Publishers:
www.publishers.org/

Publishers Weekly
www.publishersweekly.com

The Bookseller
www.thebookseller.com

Other Book Fairs
www.buchmesse.de/de/networking/ messen_
maerkte/internationale_buchmessen/

World Intellectual Property Organization
www.wipo.int/copyright/en

APPENDIX D: SUGGESTED READING

HERMAN, Jeff. *Guide to Book Publishers, Editors and Literary Agents* 2007. Massachussets: Three Dog Press, 2007.

KASDORF, William E. *The Columbia Guide to Digital Publishing.* New York: Columbia University Press, 2003.

OWEN, Lynette. *Selling Rights.* London: Routledge Chapmann & Hall, 2006.

QU, Sanqiang. *Copyright in China.* Beijing: Foreign Languages Press, 2002.

RADUNTZ, Helen. *Intellectual Property and the Work of Information Professionals.* Oxford: Chandos Publishing, 2008.

SCHIFFRIN, André. *The Business of Books.* London and New York: Verso, 2000.

Thompson, John B. *Books on the Digital Age: The Transformation of Academic and Higher Education Publishing in Britain and the United States.* Cambridge: Polity, 2005.

———. *Merchants of Culture: The Publishing Business in the Twenty-First Century.* Cambridge: Polity, 2010.

XIN, Guangwei. *Publishing in China: An Essential Guide.* Singapore: Cengage Learning, 2010.